The Threshing
The Makings of a Soldier

The Threshing
The Makings of a Soldier

Marsha and Samuel Winters

EQUIP PRESS
Colorado Springs, Colorado

The Threshing
The Makings of a Soldier

Published by Equip Press, Colorado Springs, CO

First Edition: 2018
The Threshing: The Makings of a Soldier / Marsha and Samuel Winters
Paperback ISBN: 978-1-946453-17-4
eBook ISBN: 978-1-946453-18-1

Dedication

Dedicated to Joseph, Rachel, Maria and Emmanuel.
I hope that you perfect what I've learned so that you'll be a
driving force to be reckoned with.

About The Authors

Marsha and Samuel Winters have been married for over twenty years and have been in full-time ministry for almost just as long. In that time they have four children as a reward. As an associate pastor of a small church in Long Island, NY, they have seen a lot. After ministering to thousands of people through, preachings, teachings and the arts, Marsha and Samuel have a passion to minister to those who have gone through trauma, loss or abuse. They have their own organization called, "Through the Winters." It is through this ministry the Winters aim to help individuals find purpose in their pain.

Acknowledgment

Writing this book has been very challenging. At the same time, it's been one of our most fulfilling times of ministry as well. The ability to do this work alone is just not realistic.

Sam and I truly know that if we did not have four very amazing children supporting us, this work would not have been accomplished. Thank you so much to our four blessings from Heaven for being flexible, supportive and willing to go on this journey with us. We especially appreciate how you all wish to be a part of this ministry as opposed to just sitting on the sidelines. We love you.

To Elizabeth Madaia, outside of ourselves, no one has been dedicated to this ministry more than you. You stayed up late reading and critiquing this book, giving suggestions and helped in pushing us forward. You made our goal, your goal, and invested 150% to get it done. No request was too great, no goal was too unreachable, and no vision was too crazy for you. Thank you for walking this journey with us as if it were your own. In addition, thank you for all your hard work and long days with us. This journey has just started and we are honored to have you on it with us.

Both Sam and I have the best mothers that two people could have. Your prayers and intercessions for us and our ministry has allowed us to dig deeper into who we are. We love and appreciate your support and encouragement for our endeavors. Most of all, thank you both for always being our biggest fans.

To our dear Pastor Dominick and Kathy, words cannot express the gratitude we feel for all your love and for believing in us. Pastor, it has been your willingness to let us pursue this side of ministry that has allowed us to be where we are. We know it wasn't easy at times, but your trust has been something we treasure greatly.

To Mildred and Zachary—my favorite soccer players ever—I wrote this book right in class with you. Both of you are stronger than you think. I see the soldier in both of you and I appreciate you letting me speak into your lives as a teacher and a mentor. Both of you have provided me plenty of material.

To the Badaiasons and Munchkin Ramirez we cannot explain what you guys do for us. You have redefined the word family. When we were overwhelmed with ministry you were always ready to scoop up the kids and be there for them. You took them out and loved them as your own. Thank you all for making them feel loved in more ways than one and for having us be a part of your family as well.

Imani and Roddy, your dedication to my kids has given them new views of God. Thank you for taking the time to support us and encourage us as our kid's youth pastors and family.

Last but not least, to Nicole Horstman, thank you for letting us keep Kyle alive in our way and for allowing a brief part of his story to be a large part of ours. We love you and your children. What a soldier. What a warrior. What a husband and Father. What a fighter.

Foreword

Soldiers are our heroes because they fight for everything
we hold dear: our country, our values and our lives. Some
soldiers fight on foreign ground and others fight at home,
yet not all soldiering is done in the physical realm.

As Marsha Winters tells her story, we see the parallels
of a developing soldier that is reflected in each of us. That
development comes as we weather the events of life (good and
bad) and choose to let them shape and strengthen us.

It's not the events of life that make us who we are, but
our interpretation of those events. Our response to tragedy can
make us a victim or a victor. We can be beaten down or we can
have a strengthened resolve for the next challenge.

We've all read books that give direction for living victoriously.
What makes this book different is that Sam and Marsha reach
out a hand to you and invite you to walk along with them in
their journey. They passionately share the challenge, hope, and
joy of their walk together. They have lived the journey. I know
they would say with the apostle Paul, "Follow us as we follow
Christ!"

As Marsha walks us through her development as a
soldier of the Lord, each of us can benefit from seeing similar

opportunities we have been given to make the tragedies and hurts of life into sources of strength and wisdom. May your preparation for the battles ahead bring you victories like Marsha's.

Duane P. Durst
Superintendent of the New York Ministry Network
of the Assemblies of God

Contents

Introduction

As a typical mother of four young children, I am happy when my hectic day is over. I also love to watch a nice calming movie or T.V. show with my husband to finish the day. Most women would be completely engrossed by a movie if it focused on romance or friendship; I find complete joy in the opposite. When I go out on a date with my hubby, he knows he had better not take me to a sappy movie that leaves me begging for tissues or wanting to text a friend that "I love them" because of deep emotions the movie has stirred. He knows that I prefer a movie where the star actor is walking away with flames flaring behind him from something he just blew up, or a superhero waiting for a villain to take one more step so they can lay the smack down on them. That is a good movie or television series.

One of my favorite shows was a series called, *The Unit* starring Dennis Haysbert as Jonas Blaine. I absolutely love Dennis. If I didn't have one of the most affordable car insurances in the world, I would have signed up with Allstate a long time ago just because he is their spokesman. Anyway, this show was nothing like any other action packed soldier series I have seen. It followed five men who were a secret group of soldiers put together by the president of the United States. Only a small handful of people knew what these five men really did. They masked themselves as ordinary military recruits and base workers. The "Unit" was called upon for the most secretive, dangerous and intense missions. They had to leave their families and lives at a moment's notice whenever called, unable to divulge any information of their mission or destination.

Their wives knew that they were a part of this secret sect of the military, but they were never fully brought in on what was happening, neither before, nor after a mission. They were expected to keep their husband's secrets at all cost, having only each other for support, not knowing when or if they would see their husbands again. The lack of information was also an added precaution in case the wives were ever in a compromising situation or if the husband was captured; they would have little information to give. These women developed a strong bond and comfort in each others company because of the support needed to endure the challenges of this unusual lifestyle.

In Season 1, episode 8 entitled "SERE," the Unit is getting ready for a "training drill" where they are to guard fellow soldiers who were going to pretend to be prisoners of war. They were told that the drill was to teach them new interrogation techniques and they were supposed to help the head of administration break the will of the soldiers during a "mock" setting. This training was used to see if these soldiers would break and give up National Security Intel, or any other information that would endanger other soldiers or their country.

Jonas's team got out of the van and he warned his men not to push the fake prisoners of war too far because it was just a "drill." Once they exited their vehicles the team was met with guns pointed at them and they were given orders to put their hands up. To the team's complete surprise, they quickly learned that they were not guards, but in fact the POW's (prisoners of war) themselves. In this intense episode this rock solid team was pushed to the limit in more ways than one. They were surprised at the level of torture, mind games and sabotage used to break them as a unit. In these mind games, the administration tried to play with the soldier's emotions to get them to break. One member of the team made Jonas nervous because he started this training mildly sick. This team member refused to opt out and while he was a prisoner he became severely ill. The team was separated and brainwashed to think that the ill soldier had turned on them. It got to the point where they did not know what to believe. They had been beaten up, disillusioned, and denied food and water. How were they going to overcome this?

The best part of this episode was in a scene where the Commanding Officer of the Unit was watching on a monitor all that was transpiring with the administration conducting the drill. The Commanding Officer knew that the administrators would never be able to break his men. He told them that this team was not to be compared to any other team they had come across before. They were strong, they were focused, and they would rather die in this mission than give up their country. His confidence made the leader of the school angrier and more determined. Their Commanding Officer knew them well. He knew how far they could be pushed.

The Unit showed how good they were when they were able to use the little items around them to make a blow torch and break free from their holding cell. The Commanding Officer found it absolutely hilarious as this team proved their strength, agility and dedication when they were found **outside** the school as a strong unified front. I need to remind you that this was just "training."

I often ask myself, as Christians in today's world are we as residual and dedicated as these men were to their government? If we were to be given a label by God, would He say we are dedicated and loyal to the cause of Christ, faithful, strong, unmovable, and perseverant? Jonas's company was confident in their abilities; could God say the same about his team? Or would he call us pampered, spoiled, disobedient, shallow, wimpy, cowardly, unfaithful, babies that won't grow up? I have been serving the Lord for over twenty-five years and I am inclined to agree with the latter.

If you saw me and my life at twelve years old, you wouldn't see a girl that would remind you of a character on Disney XD or Nick Junior. I was more like one of the girls you'd see making a cameo on shows like NCIS or CSI. I was a handful to those around me. Fast forward to the year 2013 when the Lord put it on my heart to write my testimony down on paper; from doing that came my first book, *The Threshing: A Weapon Forged by Fire.* This first book is where the essence of my testimony can be found. God gave me Isaiah 41:15. Though it was hard to relive many of the moments mentioned there, I wrote knowing that God was having me write so that my story could be used to help others find strength in Christ as I did. Now with this second book, I hope to do the same but in a way that will equip my readers to help the next generation.

In the United States, most, if not all, do not understand the mentality of living for God as a soldier. Jesus Christ, our Commanding Officer, knows we are in a war. This war over mankind is waged on us by Satan. I heard it said, "A soldier that won't fight is completely useless." Once we make our decision to walk with God we must get ready to fight. The problem lies in the dedication and agility of God's soldiers; He needs His soldiers to step up their game and stay focused. Satan plays for keeps. He is not playing games or shooting blanks at us.

The Threshing: The Making of a Soldier is speaking to the fighter that is in all of God's children. As a survivor of severe physical and sexual abuse I was destined for self-destruction even though I was born again. It wasn't just enough for me to ask God into my life, I needed to surrender my life over to Him. I needed to fight my way out of my past and then take my past and use it as ammo against the enemy, but it would take me listening to God's instructions so I could be that soldier, that warrior God has called all of his children to be.

We are all called to fight in this war and in this book we have to take the time to challenge our own refusal to follow God's orders. Our Commanding Officer knows the end from the beginning, he knows the best way to fight our enemy, and— even though this war is not between him and Satan—he is fighting this war with us.

I had to learn that we need to stop living for God as if we are punching a time-clock for a paid job, expecting recognition, benefits of the highest quality, appreciation and the Christian-of-the-Year Award. It does not work that way. We have to stop rubbing the Bible like it is a magic lamp, hoping to be granted three amazing wishes. This is a position held by loyal, strong, powerful, focused, dedicated, chosen people who will not be easily turned around by hard times or persecution. We are Soldiers in The Army of The Lord.

CHAPTER ONE

Soldier

I am Stronger than this challenge.
And this challenge is making me Stronger.

The junior high school years are when pre-teens venture away from that immature life they once knew in elementary school. There are no more naps, field trips to the zoo, or snacks in the middle of the afternoon. This is another level of learning and a new course of responsibilities and independence. This is junior high, the rite of passage into "teen-hood." For me, it was a chance to leave the past behind. Two years earlier, my father was called into the school because I was getting into fights and because of my constant disrespectful behavior. That was the day my father viciously beat me in front of my teachers and classmates. News of the incident spread like wild fire and it was not long before I became known as "the girl who got beaten up in the school by her father." I needed to leave that life behind me and get a fresh start. Of course there were some kids from my former elementary school attending my new school, but the school was big enough that I didn't see them much.

So one day, a day just like any other day, I found myself sitting in the principal's office. He was just sitting behind his desk looking at me. I sat there with my shirt stretched out of shape, my hair all messed up and my left eye pulsing with pain as it slowly swelled up more and more. I began to tear up as the principal just sat there, not saying a word, just staring at me as if I had two heads. I waited for his first comment so that that awkward silence could be broken. I looked at my hands and noticed that there was blood underneath my nails and it was not mine. It belonged to the boy who was sitting on the other side of the office.

A half hour before...

English class proved to be as boring as ever, so when I heard the bell for my next class, I thought to myself, "There's my salvation!" My three close friends and I grabbed our books and headed over to our next class, Science. When we got to the classroom, we were pleasantly surprised to find out that our teacher was absent and that there was a substitute. Our teacher's absence meant only one thing: the class could relax and goof-off for the next forty-five minutes. My friends and I grabbed seats that allowed us to sit right next to each other and we started talking while several of the boys stayed in the back of the classroom horsing around. Everyone behaved as if there was no teacher in the room at all.

It wasn't too long before all of us were as loud as loud could be. I don't think the substitute even tried to bother with the lesson. As I was chatting away with my friends I noticed one of the boys in my class, Gerry, staring at me. Now Gerry was twice, maybe three, times my size and I thought of him as one of the nicer guys in the class. He was never antagonizing and, for the most part, kept to himself. He barely ever said a word to me and always seemed polite. I didn't think much of his gaze until a few minutes went by and saw him still looking at me. Looking back at him across the room, I was totally taken back when he yelled out to me saying, "Yo! Marsha you're in my seat, get up now, or else I'm gonna make you get up!" Those around him started to laugh and the rest of the class stopped whatever they were doing. All eyes were on us; our classmates started whispering because they knew something was going to go down real soon. As I said, Gerry was one of the nice ones and, until now, I had never heard him threaten anyone before. For a moment I was confused when he addressed me in that manner but I took a guess at what was happening. The only thing that made sense was that the other boys had dared him to challenge me to a fight. Why me? Why not pick on someone his own size?

Now here I was, twelve years old and it was a little under six months since I had asked the Lord into my heart. I really wanted to be a good girl. I don't know if any of those boys had heard about my past or if they just thought it would be funny to pick on the small girl in the class, but at that age I was a very aggressive little girl. I had worked hard to keep from using foul language, and desperately tried to win the struggle with my bad temper. In my previous school I was known for many bad things and fighting was definitely on the top of that list. I fought only two girls my whole life; most of my confrontations were usually with boys. That was what I was known for. I don't know if Gerry knew that. I was not one to run from a fight even if it was with a boy, but this was no ordinary boy. Compared to me, Gerry looked like a short sumo wrestler. So when he said the words, "Get up now or I'm gonna make you get up!" my previous instincts tried to manifest. I felt my confusion turn to anger. I was trying desperately to be different than before but it was days like this that proved to me that it wasn't going to be an easy thing to do.

What do you think I did? Did I apologize for sitting in his seat and just get another one? Nope, I looked at the seat I was sitting in and yelled back at him, "Come make me!" The class parted like the Red Sea to give Gerry the room to "make me" get out of his seat. They knew just as much as I did that there was going to be a rumble. I look back at it now and really wonder, where in the world was the substitute teacher? Gerry jumped off the back counter where he had been sitting with the other boys and proceeded to walk towards me. I thought to myself: *"What in the world are you thinking? This guy is actually growing bigger with every step he takes, Marsha! Do you see how big this kid is? He's going to crush you."* I knew that every step he took towards me lessened my chances of running out of the classroom and saving myself. My mind was quickly running through scenarios, but I had no idea what I was going to do. My heart was racing, but running was not an option. I was going to face him and take my punches. Win or lose, I was not backing down from this fight. Oh, the pride of a twelve-year-old ex-bully. By the time Gerry got to where I was sitting I was on my feet ready for whatever was coming my way. He pushed me with all his might into a wall, grabbed my shirt, and hit me right in my eye. I saw stars just like in the Bugs Bunny Cartoons. I thought to myself: *"Marsha you've been hit, now apologize, lick your wounds and move on."* Yeah right! I was not that holy yet. God was just BEGINNING a new work in me.

As I got my bearings my survival instincts kicked in; my rage went from a two to about fifty five. I was angrier than I remember ever being and I was not going to let some punk kid get the better of me. So I turned around, jumped on him, and proceeded to hit him with all my twelve-year-old, Ninety lbs. might. When that was not bringing down the giant, I opened my hands and proceeded to slash him in the face as deep as I could with my nails. He grabbed a hold of me and tried to get me off of him, but I clung to him like a pair of really tight skinny jeans. He finally peeled me off and tried to throw me, but I grabbed him again quickly and the momentum pulled him down with me. He landed right on top of me—and believe it or not—that's exactly where I was able to finish the fight. I held tight to his shirt and continued slashing and punching him in the face as hard as I could before that invisible substitute teacher finally showed up. Even though the substitute teacher tried hard, it was the school security officers who finally pulled us apart, and sent us to the principal's office.

Back to the principal's office...

The principal finally spoke and said, "I cannot believe this." He turned to Gerry, "What are you doing hitting a girl? You are twice her size, (*LITERALLY*) and you pick a fight with her? What kind of man hits a girl?" The principal stopped and looked at Gerry's face in pure disbelief, then went on to say, "But boy she messed up your face, BAD! Have you seen your face Gerry? Have you gone to the bathroom and seen what you look like?" Gerry nodded his head. The principal continued to humiliate him by saying, "Looking at her, it seems like you got one good hit, but she made an impression on your face that will be there for a while." Gerry, completely embarrassed, did not answer. He sat there with multiple—and I mean *multiple*—slashes across his face. It looked like he got into a fight with a stray cat and lost…badly. The principal continued. "I think when you look at your face for the next month, you'll think twice before you pick another fight with this girl or any other girl." That fight with Gerry was the second to last fight I ever had. From a very young age I possessed the heart of a fighter.

The Fighter in me…

I remember shortly after my father passed away (I was fourteen years old) that my little brother Peter came home in tears because of what some boys had said to him. There was a rumor going around that my father had died of a drug overdose. Apparently the kids on the first floor of my seven story building thought it was a good idea to start these lies. My mother and I went to the apartment of these kids to speak to their parents. As much as I disliked my father, I did not want his legacy to be associated with such lies, and this bothered me a lot. My mother and the mother of the boy who started the rumors began to talk. It started off at a decent pace, but at some point in the discussion the woman began to get an attitude with my mom, and it was at that point I began to feel smoke coming from my ears. I became so full of rage that I started to mouth off at the woman. My mother was trying to quiet me down, but it did no good. The other woman told me to shut up and in an impulse I lunged forward to grab her so that I could teach her a lesson. As I write this I think of how crazy I was. My mother stood in front of me, and her attention was now on protecting this lady and getting me under control. I was a soul that needed God more than ever. There was no way that I was going to be able to survive if God did not take a hold of my life. I was a broken vessel in need of a purpose and meaning.

I fought for so many things in my life: love, justice, peace, relationships, and acceptance. It's not in my DNA to run away from a fight, and even though it sometimes causes me pain, grief, and/or embarrassment it has also provided me with some moments of joy. When I truly bowed the knee to God and accepted Him as my Lord and Savior, I willfully surrendered myself to him. I was expecting the fighter in me to leave, but surprisingly enough God loved that about me, He just needed to tame it a bit. This taming process would teach me many things, like submission and patience. It allowed me to see what was worth holding on to and what I needed to let go of. He needed me to see that my enemy was not who I thought it was and that my reasons for fighting needed to change. Before coming to accept Christ, I was using the wrong kind of weapons and depending on my own strength to win my battles. My heart has always been one of a fighter.

When I was older someone gave me a copy of the most powerful poem I have ever read. The poem is called "Soldier" and unfortunately this poem is by an "Unknown Author." The words of this poem, I feel, mirror a warrior who is focused and dedicated to their Commanding Officer who Christ. Here is a portion of that poem…

SOLDIER

I am a soldier in the army of my God
The Lord Jesus Christ is my Commanding Officer.
The Holy Bible is my code of conduct.
Faith, Prayer and the Word are my weapons of Warfare.
I have been taught by the Holy Spirit, trained by experience, tried by
adversity and tested by fire.
I will either retire in this army at the rapture or die in this Army;
but I will not get out, sell out, be talked out, or be pushed out.
I am faithful, reliable, capable and dependable.

This poem is so inspiring to me because I am a small Jamaican woman in stature. My voice could fool anyone to believe that I am passive and timid yet I can tell you that I am anything but. When I first got a hold of this poem I was in Bible College, thankfully with a new lease on life. I had been saved for seven years, and was breaking from a life of sin and insecurities. Even though I had been saved for those years, I still battled with anger, fear and had serious aggression issues. To this day, I still have some scars on my right hand as a result of punching people. By the time I reached Bible College

I had given up my life of physical fighting. I decided to give that to the Lord instead and let Him fight my battles. It didn't, however, stop me from having my moments of pure blinding rage.

When God Loves What I Hate

I remember one instance in particular when my temper got the best of me and I started to convince myself that I could never change. In my Bible School there was a small (school-run) café called "the Felly" that students worked in to fulfill their work-hour requirement. Everyone wanted to be there and I was excited to be assigned to this campus chore.

I loved going in to play my music through my radio at the top volume. It set the atmosphere and was a fun time for everyone until one unusual day. I went in as any other day and I decided to play my (non-traditional) Christian music, loud enough for the other students to enjoy themselves. It was getting late and I needed to close up. Everyone left, but one of my guy friends stayed behind to keep me company while I cleaned up.

As the empty Felly filled with my cleaning music, I was shocked by one of the professors who decided to come in to tell me to lower the music. This professor was not well-liked among the student body because of his often harsh, bitter criticism and this moment was not anything different.

He came in as if he had a fight with someone else and wanted to take it out on me. He demanded my music be shut off and then went on to look around the café to tell me what was left for me to do. He went on to lecture me with such a nasty, self-righteous attitude that it made me sick looking at him. All he needed was a white glove so he could rub his nasty finger across the desk to show where I missed.

My ears started getting hot, tears started welling up in my eyes, and my heart was beating out of my chest. I knew I was going to explode, but I had to hold it in. He then turned to my friend and started criticizing him as he grabbed a drink from the cooler and made his long road out the door.

I was afraid that I wasn't going to let him make it to the door without running across the room and tackling him like a football player in the Super Bowl. My breathing accelerated as he opened the door and walked out. I made it.

My friend asked me if I was okay, but I knew that if I spoke the words that came into my mind I would have been kicked out of the school before the sun was up. Instead, I started crying, so I grabbed the nearest plate, shattered it on the floor, and continued to throw whatever was near me. My friend thought it would be helpful to grab my hand to keep me from losing it, but that almost ended bad for him. He could tell that he needed to let me go before the situation got worse.

In *The Threshing: A Weapon Forged by Fire*, I shared a time I was in a fit of rage and started fighting a boy in the basement of a church. My friend tried to stop me. Unfortunately, I ended up beating both of them up because in my blind rage I couldn't comprehend what I was doing.

It was this incident that made me want to change the person I was. Even though I was able to think through my anger and not take my anger out on my friend in the café, I was still boiling with rage. I did not resolve my anger by having an altercation, but my aggression still did not know any other outlet but chaos. The only difference now was that instead of releasing the pain on others, I focused it on objects, but the pain within me stayed; the torment I put myself through was getting worse with each fit I had. I had no peace and I needed to change because I could not keep doing this and serve God successfully.

As I sought God more He said to me one day, "I love you *and* the fight in you. I am going to use it. I created you to be a soldier, a fighter, a warrior. I will train you to redirect your aggression to your real enemy: Satan. You will never be ordinary because I've made you extraordinary." That was while I was still in Bible College and for the next several years He has trained me to be a soldier in His army. I've had tragedies and triumphs, missteps and victories. I've both gained and lost friends and have developed some enemies as well. I have also learned, over the years, how to better hear His voice, interpret His Word and grow in His presence. To be a soldier for God comes at a price, but what you give up is small in comparison to what you get in return. *"I have been taught by the Holy Spirit, trained by experience, tried by adversity and tested by fire."* Each one of us have a past. Some of us have a past that was harder than most. We can allow our past to limit our future or we can allow it to be used as a weapon to help show others who God really is. If you choose the latter, then there is work that needs to be done, a training that needs to take place in order to teach you how to fight the right way. This training will force you to confront your past and your fears. It forces you to push yourself out of your own comfort zone in order to truly learn what it means to trust

God. You will have moments of joy and moments of tears, but all of this takes place to help you grow. In the military they call this type of training Boot Camp. It's the process one goes through to become a soldier.

Are you ready to go through God's Boot Camp? It won't always be easy, but the training you experience, I guarantee, will be worth the work.

CHAPTER TWO

Boot camp

The more you sweat in peace,
the less you bleed in war.
—Norman Schwarzkoff

Basic Training

My older brother James and I were separated for ten years when I lived in the United States and he lived in Jamaica West Indies. I was thirteen years old and James was eighteen when our family was finally reunited. The bond between my big brother and I was extremely strong, so it was very hard for me when, after just a year of our reunion, James enlisted into the Marine Corp. As awful as it was to have my brother leave for the military, the stories he shared of the many scenarios he was placed in during Boot Camp fascinated me.

For the purpose of writing this portion of the book, I sat down with him so he could tell me more about his experiences during his time in the military. I really wanted to know what boot camp was like, so I asked him if he could share with me some of his strongest memories of that time. James sat back, closed his eyes and journeyed back in his mind to the time when he first showed up on base almost twenty-five years ago.

"Well, I don't know how it is now, but when I arrived on base I was informed that even though I signed up for the Marines I was still not in boot camp. Boot camp started two weeks later. They put me through rigorous testing and training to break me *before* the real boot camp started. They preyed on the weak, Marsha. They pushed you to the limits whether it was to make you cry or even give up. They wanted to see how far they could go before you threw in the towel. There were men that did give up, but they let us know that giving up wasn't that easy. There was a consequence for giving up, but I'm not sure what it was."

I then asked him about the different exercises that were considered "training." I was blown away when he took out a book that resembled a High School yearbook with pictures of other new recruits, some showing pure agony as they are being put through strenuous drills. "Let me tell you about this training. The military wanted to make sure that we were able to endure chemical warfare if we were ever faced with it. We had to make sure that our masks were working properly, but they drilled it in us that we had to be clean shaven. They told us that even facial hair could get between parts of the mask, and let in chemicals. Even the smallest exposure could be fatal." I sat at the edge of my seat as he continued, "For our training we were all brought to a field, and were given our orders. On top of us was a helicopter that dropped chemicals on us."

"Was it a lot?" I asked shocked.

With humor in his voice, "It was enough. It was enough!" He and I busted out laughing as he continued. "There was another drill where we were inside for the chemical training. This was the moment I realized that whatever I did was going to affect everyone else. The training started and I was losing my breath. I wanted to run out of the area, but if I ran out I would have technically "killed" my whole platoon. I ran to the door and everyone in my platoon was screaming for me not to go. My drill sergeant was telling my crew to let me go." I listened intently as I thought of all those shows on television where one soldier is freaking out and his panic cost everyone their lives. "I wanted to go through the door Marsha, but I stopped. It was then that I realized I was connected to everyone in my platoon." I sat there listening to my brother with the thought in my head saying, *"They called this...TRAINING!"*

What is training for? Training is to get you into the reality that this is not a game and it cannot be treated as such. I don't think anyone really knows what they are in for when they enlist into the Army of the Lord. We have so many recruits who never make it to the real battle, simply because they give up during Boot Camp. Does God take us through boot camp? Any good leader trains his soldiers before sending them into war, right? If we know that we are led by the best leader ever then we must look at the training He provides, as preparation for battle.

Follow my thoughts here for a bit. If we were to look at our lives as if we were at war, on the day you finally bow the knee to the Lord, who is your CO (Commanding Officer), and you invite him into your heart after confessing your sins, what you have done is you enlisted yourself into His Army. In a bigger scope you've basically switched sides and defected to a different boot camp.

It isn't explained to many new believers that once we have finally decided to give our lives over to the Lord we are taken through a "boot camp" of sorts. It's not told to some that they will be faced with new ways of seeing life. It's not explained that some people who we believed we were close with, would not take kindly to the news that we are now Christian. For some bowing the knee could mean a change in their lifestyle, for others it may mean that they have to let go of things. I've learned that choosing to live this life with Christ meant that I had to let go of the image I had of myself and what I believed defined me; instead, I need to trust the person God had shown me I could be.

Who are you now?

When James left for the Marines he was totally unprepared for the things he would have to endure. Before he left for the military he was quite a disciplined and driven young man. He had a very good understanding of respect and honor, but once he arrived at boot camp he experienced a totally different perspective of what it meant to live a truly disciplined life. He realized that he was not as committed, organized or as physically in shape as he thought he was. "Marsha they get into your head," he told me. "They made you feel like trash. There were times they screamed in my face and dared me to strike them. It took everything in me not to lose my cool." Anyone who has gone through boot camp can relate to this. For James, it was literally stripping him of his ego and individuality. He had to understand that he was a part of something bigger than himself. He was a member of the platoon, a team of other soldiers, and he had to understand that every right or wrong move could possibly affect everyone else. James had a view of himself before joining the military, but all that he thought he was, changed when he signed on as a recruit.

I am so thankful that man's methods are not God's. Even though we are in a war, God does not treat us as man treats us. I get it and understand the reasoning behind the methods used; however where they belittled James and made him feel like dirt to remove his ego and pride, God finds different ways to change us. Like my brother, I came to God full of ego and pride and even though I was saved, I still believed that I was calling the shots. I was cocky, arrogant, self-centered and so much more.

When I was fifteen years old my mother surrendered her heart to the Lord. You would think that her salvation would have given me satisfaction, but for some reason I felt superior to her, because I saw her as the "new Christian" and I was the more experienced. As I watched her change her life for the better, I grew angry and even jealous. She desired God and His words so much and she was willing to let go of whatever was hindering her relationship with God. What seemed so easy for her didn't come that way for me and I didn't understand why. I was "saved" much longer than her and yet my struggles still remained in me. Sadly, I made this period of my mother's life more than a bit difficult. Not only was she my mother, but now she was also my sister in Christ. I, however, was more interested in myself. Instead of sharing in her journey I made it all about me. I needed God to strip away my pride before I could be considered a soldier in His Army. If I continued in this behavior and thinking, my pride was surely going to destroy me.

Whether you want to believe it or not we have an enemy who does not want us to be enlisted in the Lord's Army. Satan thrives on our pride because he knows that it is a key component in keeping us from winning the battle. Our enemy loves the fact that we are ignorant of his hand and presence in our lives. This ignorance creates bondage in our minds, our spiritual growth, and so much more; all without our knowledge that any of it is even happening.

> *"I beg you that when I come I may not have to be as bold as I expect to be toward some people who think that we live by the standards of this world. For though we live in the world, we do not wage war as the world does. The weapons we fight with are not the weapons of the world. On the contrary, they have divine power to demolish strongholds."*
> **2 Corinthians 10:2-4**

I have no doubt in my mind that if we were able to see in a physical form the hold the enemy had over us, all the preparation that God puts us through would be so appreciated. Though we may not see all that goes on around us, God does and even better, He knows what we need to fight back. We complain so quickly that it's too hard and that there are so many rules, but we say those things not realizing the war around us.

Nothing but a piece of clay

In the Marines, James explained that the drill sergeants would scream and make them do push-ups and other exercises to help strengthen the recruits for what was to come. Though, at first, it all seemed heartless and excessive, it was all needed to strip away the egos and individuality of each future soldier. In the book of Jeremiah, God expresses to the prophet His hopes for the nation of Israel if they would trust Him.

> *This is the word that came to Jeremiah from the* LORD; *"Go down to the potter's house, and there I will give you my message." So I went down to the potter's house, and I saw him working at the wheel. But the pot he was shaping from the clay was marred in his hands; so the potter formed it into another pot, shaping it as seemed best to him. Then the word of the* LORD *came to me. He said, "Can I not do with you, Israel, as this potter does?" declares the* LORD. *"Like clay in the hand of the potter, so are you in my hand, Israel."*
> **Jeremiah 18: 1-6**

Coming from a past where sexual and physical abuse was common, the last thing I needed in my life was God screaming at me to remind me of how small a fish I was in his big pond of life, so I'm glad that He does things a little different. His reasons behind the methods used though are the same: to strengthen, develop, refine and to make aware. No matter how much I wanted to, I was not able to see myself the way God saw me. In fact when I was older, God told me that He had called me to the nations and that He would use my struggles and testimony to set others free. My problem with that was, "How could I do what God was calling me to do, when I was still battling with so much of my own insecurity?" There is a line in the Jeremiah scripture that helped me to begin to understand.

"...the clay was marred in his hands..."

The Greek definition of "marred" is to destroy, devastate, or ruin. The Lord saw me and saw that I was destroyed. He saw that I was completely devastated and ruined, but I was right where I needed to be for Him to use me, I was in *His* hands. Be honest, we all come to God in destroyed, devastated, ruin state. No one truly comes to God whole, else we wouldn't think we need God. If we turned to something or someone else for help, there would be no hope for us. In the hands of the Potter, we are more than just a lumpy piece of destroyed, useless clay.

He sees what He can form and shaped us into. God knows that there are things He needs to do with you and me and it may be hard, but when we truly allow ourselves to be in His hands our purpose and future is more defined.

"...so the potter formed it into another pot..."

You see, I believe that when we are born physically we are also born with a calling over us. This calling is given to us by the Lord. Whether we choose to follow this calling or not, Satan has his plan as well. His plans for us are to be as far from God as possible. This can be done by keeping us busy with life, or having us angry at God for all the bad things that go on around us. Whatever it is, he works hard to keep us too preoccupied to respond to God's love. Satan's plans for me could have been to make me a woman so deep in sin that I would eventually destroy myself, and along with that, any future happiness that I was destined to have.

Satan knows of the potential greatness in all of us, this is why one of his known attributes in scripture is that of a liar. He sees the talent, the strength and the danger in each of us, so he has us believe lies about God, our lives and our purpose. He sets us up in a "fun house" full of distorted mirrors and gets us to believe that we are weak, inferior, powerless and out of control good-for-nothings. Scripture records an instance where Jesus tells Simon Peter—one of His disciples—of the enemy's intentions to snuff out all the disciples.

> *"Simon, Simon, Satan has asked to sift all of you as wheat. But I have prayed for you, Simon, so your faith may not fail. When you have turned back, strengthen your brothers."* **Luke 22: 31, 32**

Satan asked God if he could sift all the disciples like wheat. The devil knew that these men could make major changes in this world and it would last forever. Likewise, he knows that you and I hold the same potential within us. The enemy knows that we are called to be warriors and fighters for the Kingdom. With me, he convinced me that I needed to aim my anger and hate towards myself and anyone else who came near me. He kept me focusing on my failures and shortcomings. When I was younger, I was so tangled with disgrace and shame triggered by my sexual addiction that I felt worthless. With this "whirlwind" of things happening, how could I ever sober up and start doing the right things?

Well there was one thing that I realized when I got older, despite his lies about my life, Satan could not change who God designed me to be. He could not change my potential, my calling, nor my purpose. The only thing in his arsenal was to distort my perspective of myself; this way he could distract me from the truth. God made me a fighter, but I was fighting the wrong enemy. He made me passionate, but my passion was not focused on what it needed to be focused on.

What has the enemy distorted about your image? Are you currently trying desperately to get out of this funhouse of mirrors that highlights your problem areas and erase your potential? God wants to break every mirror that distorts who he has created you to be.

Know who you are

My friends, God has personally shaped and molded you. He is your Creator and He knows how great you are going to be, but we may not see what He sees right away. As such, we have to trust the Father's hands. We need to believe that He knows what we need to survive on the battlefield. As I started to surrender my life to God, He started molding and forming me into a new vessel. He didn't change me into something totally different; He just made me over and helped point me in the right direction.

Many of us have things that we do not like about ourselves. We may neglect to see it could be what we dislike about ourselves that God is going to use for His Kingdom. I was a fighter, and my passions were aimed at wrong desires, but God didn't take that away from me. Instead, He showed me how to fight on His terms and be passionate about what He was passionate about. Who we are is what God created us to be, but at the same time we must make sure that the emotions and passions, as well as the desires and talents that we possess, remain in line with how He created us to be.

"...shaping it as seemed best to him."

I think this area is one that is hard and maybe even bothers all of us in one way or another. The truth is, the reshaping of our lives from our sinful nature can be hard. Imagine yourself playing with a piece of Play-Doh. You decide to shape the dough into a pancake so you take it from the container and start to mold it into what you intend it to be. What must you do in order for it to become that pancake? You squeeze it, press it, knead it, and even pound it, until it takes the form of what you intended it to be. This is why when it comes to God and us, the word "shaping" may not go well. When we think of God molding us to make us into *His* image, we know that this might mean a very unpleasant process. It is true for many that when they first surrender their lives to God's will, it has some painful moments. Sadly, they don't finish their spiritual boot camp.

As stated earlier, my brother James told me that he was placed in situations that would resemble real life situations for when he was placed in battle. They ran scenarios on him and his team exposing him to the reality of chemical warfare. He had to follow their orders and he knew that if one person messed up the whole team could be affected and hurt.

In addition to being shaped, many have a problem with the, *"as seemed best to Him"* part. No one really likes being out of control. I think there are some people who can relate with me. We want a vote and the reality is, soldiers don't get to vote. Life in the military is not a democracy, it's a dictatorship and so is the life of walking with God. There is no debating His ways and His laws. I needed to learn to trust and believe His ways were best. Be honest with me, how many of us have argued with God during the molding process because we feel like our ways are best? I know I did for a long time. We constantly criticize the work of the Potter because we think He is making mistakes. We demand to be vases when He's called us to be plates or cups. We try to put our design before Him and we get upset when He doesn't follow what we consider to be the perfect blueprint.

I was in Bible College when God told me about using my story for the nations. I had to learn that if I wanted to get the enemy back for all he did to me, I had to first learn how to follow my leader. I could not command my Commander. One of the saddest things I have witnessed is watching believers die on the proverbial battlefield because they refuse to obey orders. They are so bent on doing their own thing and following their own will, they fall into the traps laid out by the enemy. Just like the clay in the potter's hand, will we not let God do what He wills? Are we not **His** to do with what He pleases anyway? In the upcoming chapters I am going to challenge the minds of all those chosen to be in this Army. We have to stop thinking of our walk with God as a summer camp and come to the reality that this is ***Boot Camp!!*** We are required to look at life differently if we are to survive this war of "man" verses "Satan." God chose you because He knew that you were a fighter, and that you were going to be crucial to this battle. So are you ready? Are you ready to see what our Commanding Officer has in store for us?

CHAPTER THREE

Know Your Leader

Leaders become great not because of their power but,
because of their ability to empower others.
–John Maxwell

O ne of my all time favorite movies to watch is "Patriot" with Mel Gibson and the late Heath Ledger. The movie takes place at the beginning of the American Revolutionary War. Gabriel, (Heath Ledger) is of age to sign up for the war and his father Benjamin, (Mel Gibson) is pleading with him not to enlist. Gabriel goes against his father's wishes and believes that his father's plead for him not to enlist is because Benjamin is weak and a coward. As the story progresses Benjamin himself eventually enlists' into the war and is leading Gabriel's troop. Gabriel continues to see his father as weak, but as time goes by his view of his father changes when he sees his father in battle and he hears of how the other men respect him. Benjamin is not just his father, he is his Commanding Officer and he is anything but weak.

It isn't long before Gabriel discovers why his father is so revered by the other men. Benjamin was once one of the most skilled, feared and the deadliest warriors of his time. There were stories told of how he had fought when he was a soldier many years before. His killing spree was so high that Benjamin himself was ashamed and vowed never to kill like that again. Story after story, Gabriel learned of his father's bravery and skills on the battlefield. In the end Gabriel was honored to serve under his father and his army.

Do you know your leader?

I have often heard people comment and mistakenly see God in a similar way that Gabriel saw his father. They see God as passive and distant. He is interpreted, at times, as an entity who commands his own children not to fight back and instead pose as door mats for all to step on. Recently, Christians have been seen as powerless cowards who walk around mindlessly obeying meaningless orders from an imaginary friend and spewing out rhetoric that we are not sure of themselves. They see us as people who have an empty life and who hold on to a false hope of life for eternity in an imaginary heaven.

My husband is a very kind-hearted man who would not hurt a living thing on purpose. He is very patient and tries his best to see the good in people. It is one of the main reasons why some people respect and trust him, but it is also the reason why others see him as a push over. When people first meet him they don't think that right away—due to the fact that he is 6'6" and is built like a football player. What's funny is that he has a brother who is a bit bigger than him, who possesses the same loving and caring qualities. When it comes to me, though, people pick up right away that I am the opposite of Sam. I'm no longer as quick tempered as I was, but I still need to work on the art of being slow to speak, if you know what I mean. Anyway, the moment you meet Sam, you quickly see his soft and gentle side. Many assume that they can say or do whatever they want to him and he will just allow it.

As I said, he can be very patient, but there is one line he will not let you cross and that is with his family. My husband has been verbally attacked and many have challenged him to fight, but most of the time he was able to avoid confrontation and just walk away. On the other hand, come against his wife, children, mother or anyone he considers close and dear… well…you will see a whole different side.

Some years ago, as youth leaders, we found ourselves in the middle of a dilemma with the leader of our church who was over us. This leader was emotionally and mentally abusive to those he was over and he used threats to get his way. He manipulated people to do what he wanted and used his position in the church as a reason to control others. I was not one of his favorites because he could not manipulate or intimidate me. I did not agree with things he did and I did not hide my thoughts which made this leader dislike me more and more. This leader made Sam cringe every single time we had to go to church. It's sad, but we tried every way possible to avoid seeing him any time we had ministry. In fact our ministry was at times unstable and overwhelming because we needed to work with him and we never knew what was going to happen next with him.

One day my husband and I were called into a meeting by this leader and he felt that it was necessary to bring up a lot of things that he did not like about us, namely me. He began to reprimand me about the way I was with my husband, and he began to belittle my character. "I wanted to talk to both of you because it has come to my attention that there are some things going on and I can't allow it to go on anymore. First off, Marsha, I found and read your testimony, and I am appalled by the things you talk about." He was referring to a copy I had made of my testimony which I used to share with those in my church at a special meeting. It was the first time I had publicly shared some of the most personal moments of my life, but felt it was time to use it to help others break through their struggles from their past. He now was using my own words to shame me. "No one needs to know about these things. It is very clear to me that you must still struggle with lust." I sat there biting my lip, trying to keep from giving him several pieces of my mind. He continued, "How could you not be struggling with lust after going through what you went through? I have arranged for you to see a counselor of my choosing for counseling. This is the only way I'll allow you to stay in ministry here."

I interjected and said, "I have already gone to counseling."

"I don't care. You will go to a counselor of *my* choosing," he said arrogantly.

This was his play, do as I say or you no longer serve in ministry here. Now when I am in a meeting like this I want to listen to everything being said so I can get the gist of the conversation, but Sam saw what he was doing and he was trying really hard not to say anything. This leader was not done with us; he went on to say, "The main reason I called you both here is to address the way you are." (He was speaking to me.) "You are very manipulative and it is clear by the way you speak to your husband that something is wrong with you and we need to address it." He continued to imply that I was abusive to Sam.

I was beside myself. "What are you talking about?!" I asked shocked.

"A woman overheard the way you were speaking to Sam one day and she came to me. It was despicable the way you were talking to him and I am convinced that you are controlling over your husband."

"What!!" Sam said. "That is not true. When was this?" Sam blurted out impatiently.

"Well there are a few accounts that have come to my desk and I just think that this is an example of your controlling personality Marsha. You are intimidating and people are afraid of you. You are very confrontational and when it comes to you and Sam, I cannot let this go on anymore." He tried to make it sound like he was defending Sam's honor and even tried to tell Sam to admit that he was right.

As he explained the instance that the woman mentioned a bit more, Sam spoke out, "I remember that day!" he said with a crack in his voice which I knew meant he was trying to stay calm. "It was right after youth group and I was suffering with a really bad migraine. I could barely stand up straight but there were still kids who didn't have a ride home. Marsha was trying to get me to let someone else to drop off the kids because I was so sick. I didn't want to ask anyone at the last minute and put them out. She did yell at me, but it wasn't in a controlling way, she was worried about me and wanted me to go home."

You could see that this leader didn't buy the story. "Yeah?" He said sarcastically.

"Yes that is what happened. You're wrong. Why didn't you just ask me, why the whole lecture? I feel like you're using this to attack Marsha."

The leader continued to try and counsel my husband like he was an abused husband in denial, "Sam I know you are a loving man but it's your wife; your wife needs to be stopped. I see how she treats you and..." before he could finish my husband lost his teddy bear attributes and became a grizzly.

"WHO DO YOU THINK YOU ARE!! YOU HAVE NO RIGHT TO TALK ABOUT HER THAT WAY!!!"

He was shocked by the tone of Sam's voice. "Pastor Sam you need to lower your voice."

"NO!!" Sam bellowed. "How dare you take my wife's testimony and sit here and attack her like this!!" He was getting louder and louder. To me it was like he was growing.

I interjected, "Sam calm down!" I was trying to get him to keep from losing his cool, but it was too late. Now that the leader had lost his control in the meeting he had the audacity to tell me to control my husband. "Does it look like he is listening to me right now?" I was both tickled by his pure stupidity and unsure of what to do?

Sam kept going, "It is one thing for you to come after me and attack me, I can deal with that, but it is another thing for you to come after my WIFE!!" My 6'6" 300 plus pound husband stood to his feet and slammed his fist on the desk bringing real fear on the face of this leader and me, I'll admit. I didn't know what he was going to do. I had not see this anger, even in our own tussles.

"YOU NEED TO CALM DOWN!!" This leader said jumping back and to his feet in shock. "Marsha control him!"

I found complete enjoyment in this as I said, "Who is the one in control now??"

"Leave my wife alone! You don't talk to her anymore." Sam said firmly. I know my husband wouldn't have crossed the line—this man and his pathetic attacks weren't worth it but I proceeded to push my husband out the door to calm him down.

You see *I* knew just by the way we were approached before this meeting, that something was up. After reflecting on the meeting and the words said, it was obvious that we were being set up and that this leader had an agenda. He planned on my husband's kind demeanor to be the way in which he would divide us. He threatened our ministry if we did not do things his way. Sadly, this very unwise man was unaware that—though my husband was a good, kind person—he also had limits and coming against his wife was number one. This leader assumed that he knew my Sam because of the times he saw him in passing, but if he had really taken the time to know him, he would have approached the situation in a completely different manner. If he had approached us as a loving, caring and concerned leader, instead of in such an accusatory manner, the result would have been more satisfactory for all concerned.

My "gentle" God

As I grow more in my faith, I feel like many do the same thing when it comes to God and His patience. So many forget that when someone God loves is attacked, there are major consequences. We talk about each other with forked tongues, gossiping, backbiting and destroying reputations believing that God will just sit back and let the entire thing take place with no repercussion.

Maybe you are on the other side of the coin and have been the one on the victim's end. People's attacks have you feeling that God is sitting there hearing everything but doing nothing. This is one of the many reasons why just knowing of God is not enough. Just knowing "of" God can cause one to question everything that goes on. It can cause us to doubt His willingness to protect, and strength in our lives. To be a true follower of God is not to just know of Him, but to "follow Him." That means to learn about Him through His Word, seek His wisdom, guidance in times of prayer, dedicate and use our lives to reflect His glory.

Like Gabriel, from the movie—who did not really know and understand why his father would not fight—he came to his own conclusion about his father, a coward. After learning more and experiencing for himself what it was like to follow Benjamin, he understood the reasons behind his father's actions.

If Sam did not take kindly to someone he cared for being attacked, you best believe that God is not in the habit of allowing others to harm his children. Look at what happens when David was in need and he called on God for help. Take a minute to read all of this amazing chapter, but these are my favorite verses...

> ⁶ *In my distress I called to the* LORD; *I cried to my God for help.From his temple he heard my voice; my cry came before him, into his ears.* ⁷ *The earth trembled and quaked, and the foundations of the mountains shook; they trembled because he was angry.* ⁸ *Smoke rose from his nostrils; consuming fire came from his mouth, burning coals blazed out of it.* ⁹ *He parted the heavens and came down; dark clouds were under his feet.* **Psalms 18vs 6-9**

This is crazy! To paraphrase, "When I was being attacked, I called on my Daddy and He came to my rescue. God was so upset that I was being attacked, He parted the heavens to save me."

Most of us know the story of Jesus being arrested. Judas, one of Jesus' disciples, had kissed Jesus on the cheek in betrayal so that the guards would know who to take away. Jesus surrendered peacefully, but Peter impulsively pulled out his sword and cuts off an ear of one who was there to arrest Jesus. Jesus commands him to put his weapon away and goes on to say, "Do you think I cannot call on my Father and he will at once put at my disposal more than twelve legions of angels?" If you are not aware, one legion is about 6,000 or more angels. Jesus was basically saying at that moment he could ask his Heavenly Father to dispatch over 72,000 angels to destroy those arresting him but he was *letting* them capture him. *(Matt 26:50-54)*

Many have forgotten the true nature of our God and who He really is. They have adopted an insensitive, disrespectful, arrogant attitude towards Him. God sent his Son Jesus Christ to die on the cross, so that we may be forgiven for our sins. Now let me ask you. Which one of us would allow our beloved child to be tortured beyond human imagination for the benefit of others? How would you react to someone spitting in the face of your child? I don't think anyone of us would be able to do it. And yet, here it is the biggest example of the Father's love, laying down His life so that we can forever have a way to be connected to God. It was an act that not just forgave our sins, but it also allowed us the opportunity to come to Him ourselves and develop a personal relationship with God the Father.

Not long ago at a women's meeting in my current church, the women's leader explained it this way, "The same God of the Old Testament is the same God of the New Testament. God did not replace himself with a newer version of himself in Jesus Christ. He just made full provisions for escape from his wrath in the end through Jesus Christ." She continued by saying that the same God described in Psalms 18, is still the same God who watched his Son being beaten, tortured, and crucified.

It may not seem like it at the time of our struggle, but He is watching. He is recording and jotting down the wrongs and He will vindicate. Don't underestimate God's timidity and silence as a sign of weakness. Don't be fooled by the fact that he seems gentle and think that He can be manipulated. No, He knows all and sees the beginning from the end.

There are believers who have forgotten who it is that we are serving, and what kind of Commanding Officer we are following. They forget that His ways are higher than our ways and His thoughts are higher than out thoughts. They forget that He is not to be mocked and that by the mention of His name, demons tremble! Every knee will bow and *every* tongue will confess that Jesus Christ is Lord!! That is the kind of Commanding Officer we are following.

He protects His own

One of the things I have learned in serving God is how protective He is over his own. He will fight with us and for us. In my first book I shared stories of several altercations I was in when I was younger. My brother Peter, who is seven years younger than I, was so quiet and passive that he would not speak. It was not until four years of age that he really started to communicate to others and even then, it was rare. As a matter of fact (even as an adult) so many years later, Peter is still a man of very few words. Anyway, bullies felt that he was a perfect target because he was so quiet. One summer, just before I turned ten, Peter and I went to a community camp together. We were separated for most of the time. I noticed that there were some kids who were picking on him. I intervened and made it known that if anyone placed a finger on my brother, they would have to deal with me.

One of the counselors came to me with an attitude and told me that I needed to mind my own business and let my brother fight his own battles. I was very shocked at her response to my protectiveness over my baby brother. My response to her was not nice at all, "He *is* my business. As long as I live and breathe I will always fight for him. He is *my* brother and I will not let anyone put their hands on him. I don't care what you think, I will fight for him." Needless to say my counselor was aggravated at my fresh mouth and I know that if I was a little older she would have cleaned my clock.

I no longer approve of fighting, but try to see my point here. If I, as a human being, could so viciously protect my brother—even at such a young age—how much more could our God, our Father, our Commanding Officer do when His own is being attacked? I have learned the reason why He says that we are supposed to pray for our enemies. Remember the same God who loves is also the God who vindicates.

We serve a God who is slow to anger, patient and merciful; however once His wrath is provoked you will realize that we have gone too far, and God shows us that He does not take kindly to those who mess with His own. Some people take the "slow to anger" part of God as weakness, but I feel like that's actually one of the scariest parts of God. The longer it takes for God to repay someone for the evil they have done, the worse it will be.

Case in point, think about the Egyptians and the Israelites; it took 400 years for God to repay the Egyptians for the evil they had brought to the Israelites. The Egyptians had built their empire on the backs of God's people. They cheated and mistreated these people, but the worst of it was when the numbers of the children of Israel grew so much that the Egyptians started killing all the Israelite baby boys. When God had had enough, He gave Moses orders to move forward with revenge. However, God told Moses that this would not be easy, because He was going to harden Pharaoh's heart so that he would not set the Israelites free. When judgment finally came to the Egyptians they were in total shock. God could have easily wiped out Pharaoh, but He dragged it out on purpose. God sent plague after plague on this powerful empire that literally brought them to their knees. These episodes of judgment left this dominant group of people destroyed and in ruins. He ravaged their lands, destroyed their livestock, and brought down their daring leader.

God, who keeps his promises, did exactly what He said He would do. The last act of judgment was killing the first born in every family if there wasn't lamb's blood on the door. Pharaoh was broken with grief as he held his own firstborn son lifeless in his arms. When Pharaoh's pride would not allow him to leave God's children alone, God opened a body of water that was about 1398 miles long, 220.6 miles wide and 7254 feet deep to swallow a measly human being and his tiny army up mercilessly.

So, when you look around and are tempted to question why God is allowing Christian genocide, the beheading of the children of Christians, the rape of mothers and the hanging of fathers in Iraq, you need to pray for that nation. The retribution that God brought on the Egyptians should be an example that should scare us straight and beg for mercy for our enemies. If God did this to the Egypt because they persecuted the Israelites for only 400 years, what will He do to a world that has been persecuting Christians for over 2000 years? The longer it takes for God to repay evil, the worse the final attack on our enemies will be. If you don't believe me try reading the book of Revelation:

> *Then I heard a loud voice from the temple saying to the seven angels, "Go, pour out the seven bowls of God's wrath on the earth."* **Revelation 16:1**

Not one bowl, but *seven* bowls of pure organized wrath was poured out. Some battle with the book of Revelation because of the description of God's judgment in it. It may not even make sense to us because we wonder how mankind will endure such attacks. We can't accept that God could bring upon such dread and despair on mankind. God is not turning a blind eye my friend. He is patiently waiting for repentance from those who have rejected him. We must have faith in the leader we are following and trust that every decision He makes is for the good of those that love Him.

CHAPTER FOUR

What Does It Take to Be a Soldier?

The two most important days of your life is the day you were born and the day you find out why.
- *Albert Einstein*

M y husband and I just finished watching the season finale of *24: Live Another Day*. Jack Bauer is another one of my Hollywood favorites and for obvious reason. If you are not familiar with this television icon, let me fill you in a little bit. Jack has worked for the Counter Terrorist Unit for several years and during that time he has been successful in, sometimes single handedly, aborting assassination attempts on the President of the United States, a chemical attack on America or a bombing by terrorists. There have even been times, many times (almost every time) when Jack has had to go against protocol to save the lives of the American people. Bauer has been tortured time and time again; he has been captured by the Chinese, the Russians and other vengeful nations because of his success in exposing their plans. The truth is that no human being could go through what he had gone through and stay alive, but let's not focus on the negative. Let's stay with the complete action packed, nail biting, edge of your seat fantasy, real life drama.

Let me tell you a secret, sometimes I like to listen to the news and when I hear that a terrorist attack was intercepted before anything could happen, I imagine that Jack was the one who did it—I can dream can't I? One of the things I love about Jack is that he never makes threats, he only makes promises. I can't even count the numerous times he was chained up, beaten half to death, and his last words were, "I'm going to kill you." The first thought that comes to my mind is: *How in the world is he going to do that?* The enemy holding Jack hostage always finds his words senseless, unrealistic and laughable. I usually say, "Oh man, you better run now. He's comin' for ya!" Unfortunately none of the villains ever listen to my advice and they challenge Jack more—they have to or else there wouldn't be too much of a series. I'm always screaming, "Run! Run now!!" Needless to say Jack always breaks free and before the finale he has delivered on his threat to all his enemies and Jack gets to live another day.

I think I like Jack so much because he reminds me of one of my favorite people from the Bible, David. He was like the Jack Bauer in the olden days. David was outrageous, radical and totally spontaneous in so many amazing ways. There are so many reasons I look up to him, not just because of his successes, but because of his failures as well. He was a fighter that put fear into the minds and hearts of his enemies. He was strong, determined and focused on his mission, but we will talk a lot more about that part later.

What is even more amazing about David was that he had men around him with the same fire. Several years ago I read one of the most powerful books written called, *In a Pit With a Lion On a Snowy Day* by Mark Batterson. In this inspiring book Batterson highlights one of David's warriors named Benaiah. Look at what the scriptures said about him.

> *²⁰ Benaiah son of Jehoiada, a valiant fighter from Kabzeel, performed great exploits. He struck down Moab's two mightiest warriors.* ***He also went down into a pit on a snowy day and killed a lion.*** *2 Samuel 2:20*

What in the world?? Who does that? It's one of those sentences that we read and, because those words don't compute, we keep reading and figure that there must have been a typo. Batterson uses his book to focus on the truth that this man randomly went into a pit, a perfect place for a lion to maul a man, and killed this lion on a snowy, possible, icy day. Again, who does that!? You want to know who does that, a mighty warrior like Benaiah.

I recommend this book for anyone who knows they are the underdog in this game called, "life", and you want to defy odds. It was this book that played an integral part in me putting my testimony into a book. When I read the words in this book I started seeing myself the way God saw me. I was so encouraged that I did a bible study with my young adults on it. Many of them went on to do some amazing things as they took on the challenge of seeing themselves the way God did.

Benaiah was a warrior, David was a warrior. Not every soldier sees combat, but every warrior has seen and faced battle. He has learned not just by how he was trained, but also by what he has experienced. My questions to you are, "What does it take for you to be a great Soldier?" and "What battles must you face that will eventually turn you into a warrior?"

"I am committed"

How many of us can admit that we are babies when it comes to dedication? Some cry over the silliest things and need people to rub their backs or give them a high five when they do something. I cannot count how many people I have talked with, who have whined, cried and left the church for the simplest and silliest of reasons.

My husband and I have spoken to a fair share of church goers who have stopped attending because they were bitter and upset that no one called them after not being in church for two weeks. They were mad because no one came to visit them in the hospital, but they didn't tell anyone they were in the hospital to begin with. Seriously, I am so fed up with wimpy, weak spirited, needy, flaky Christians that give real believers a bad name. Man up! We allow our feelings to get so easily hurt that we can't even serve God with everything in us anymore. Our salvation and roles in the church mean nothing unless we are treated like a VIP. I am tired of spiritually breastfeeding adult believers.

Sam tries hard to seek God for his messages on Sunday mornings, and I can't tell you how many times he questions how the congregation will handle a challenging word. There have been moments where he was straight-forward and, to many, it could be thought of as harsh. We are supposed to be more than conquerors, but some of us are just bickering, nitpicking toddlers who refuse to grow up. When will we become committed to God's will and not our own? When will we recognize that all the nonsense of this world only distracts us from our true purposes in life?

I can easily talk about those whom we have met that were slackers, babies, petty and abusers of God's call and grace, but that wouldn't benefit us much. Instead I want to tell you about the relentless, dedicated, focused warriors that leave a positive impact that is not easily forgotten.

Our precious Kyle

Five years ago our church was in a big need for our members to step up and help out in our children and youth ministries. My husband's heart was bleeding as we watched our children being overlooked week after week. Sam came home angry, upset, disappointed and frustrated because there was nothing that neither he nor the other leaders could do as they watched the children's ministry slip. We needed help and we needed it fast.

One day Sam came home talking about a man who just kind of showed up to our church that was helping with the kids. His daughter was four years old—like my own daughter—so we kind of understood why he was there, but he wasn't just there—he was involved, engaged and passionate to see the kids taken care of. He not only eventually knew all the kid's names, allergies, hang ups and habits, but if something was wrong with a child he knew why and what to do to subside their anxiety. Kyle soon became our churches saving grace in children's ministry.

Sam soon became attached to him as his dry humor, quirky, introverted personality was so easily loved and admired. Eventually, Sam made up in his mind that he was going to trust Kyle and take the children's ministry in a new direction with Kyle (and another member) leading it. He became someone that my husband could rely on, but that would soon change.

Kyle and my husband found a quirky unexpected friendship with each other; their love for God, superheroes, videogames and Star Wars was a brotherhood made in Heaven. They began working together closely on a plan to help improve the churches ministry for children, but right when they were about to start this new plan it was discovered that Kyle had a cancer-like mass in his intestine. The initial diagnosis caused Kyle to be gone for a couple of months and it was then discovered that it was in fact cancerous.

Kyle dealt with the diagnosis better than anyone that I had ever met. He was more irritated that he had cancer, than heartbroken. His trust in God mirrored some of the great patriots of the Bible and nothing was rocking his faith. What bothered him the most was not the disease; however it was the fact he was missing Sundays that he was scheduled to do Children's Church. He constantly apologized for the days he missed and needed to find a replacement. On the days he could show up, he was still in pain, and in some cases he couldn't move much, yet it was his day and he was going to be there. He made those who called out, because they had the sniffles, look pathetic and weak.

The worst day for Kyle was when he spoke to Sam and expressed his frustration and resentment, as he realized that his recovery wasn't going to be as easy as he thought, and he had to take a more permanent leave from the ministry. Kyle was determined to get better because he did not want to miss one more Sunday morning, mid-week children's ministry or VBS meeting than he had to. He was the definition of committed. It was said that when Kyle came in to work with the kids he would admit to them and the other helpers when the day was a struggle. His pain reminded him of his limitations, still when he was surrounded by the children, he forgot his ailments. When he was able to do what he loved, he left stronger than when he came in.

Kyle's battle got worse as the cancer soon moved to a part of his nerve that was attached to his leg. He needed surgery and it left him in so much pain. His only way to get around was with a wheelchair. He knew that he couldn't do the children's ministry, yet the only thing on his mind was getting to church. I remember the day I saw him leaving the service, walking (because he refused to be in the chair). He was frail and weak but this cancer was not getting to his spirit. I ran to him and gently kissed his face. We talked and made jokes; not once did he complain about his condition. He simply said that he was determined to get better no matter what.

Sam's love for him grew more and more as he spent time with him at home and, at times, in the hospital. Sadly, Kyle's body started to deteriorate. He became weaker and was unable to eat. Though his body began to fail more and more, his heart did not. Kyle was not going to defeat his battle against cancer the way we all wanted him to.

Four days before his passing my husband went to visit him and Kyle was suffering and barely coherent. He could barely open his eyes and communicate; however there was one unforgettable moment that Kyle's wife told Sam about. She said that the other day Kyle lifted up his weak, frail arms and was making a strange motion with them as if he was driving. Nicole, his wife, asked "What are you doing Kyle?"

"I'm driving to help Mrs. Karen with Missionettes (Our mid week girls program)." My husband's heart broke. Four days before passing away he was going to the one place on earth that he loved being at the most, being with the children of our church to fulfill his commitment. His body wouldn't let him but his mind was right where it needed to be.

Sadly, on April 26, 2017 Kyle went to be with the Lord leaving behind a large number of people who admired him for his love, his selfless acts of kindness and commitment to God and our children.

God is attracted to those who are committed to him. Unfortunately, persecution, suffering and struggles are all a part of this walk and if we are going to give up when things are not going our way, then how can we be depended upon when the real war is waged? God has called us to be fighters, but we are also called to be committed. As soldiers, nothing must stop us from facing the enemy. We may not know all the "whys", but sometimes it is not our place to know. We need to push forward and trust in God as our leader.

I can do all things through Christ

Some years ago I saw an infomercial about facial products. I was battling at that time with severely dry skin and the thought of using soap was out of the question. I tried all these different products but none was consistent in the required results. This infomercial was so infectious that I wanted to try this product, especially since I got thirty days risk free and if I did not like it I could return it. Five years later I was still using this product and it was still working so great that two of my friends and my mother started commenting on how good my skin looked. They talked about the texture and the way it "appeared" flawless. They allowed me to treat their faces one night and they felt the difference in their skin immediately. It was then I was able to tell them about the products.

Isn't that exactly how we are supposed to be for God? We are to be like an advertisement of His strength, His mercy, and grace. If we lived as positive and effective infomercials for God, others would come to Him just by our advertisement.

I used the product on my face for several years and as my problem areas became less visible, others started asking about it. I did not announce what I did. I didn't wear a tee-shirt. I didn't get a tattoo on my arm or a bumper sticker on my car saying what I did. I just used the product the way I was told to and the affects became noticeable enough for people to ask questions.

One day Sam and I watched a six part series by Jimmy Evans called, "Indestructible Marriage." In one of his messages he said something that I will not forget. He likened our walk with God, to an advertisement. He asked the couples listening if our lives were an infomercial of what God could do for others. In other words, was our marriage one that emulated what God designed marriage to look like and was it people would want?

In times of weakness, fear, or uncertainty, many Christians recite a certain passage from the Bible time and time again, *"I can do all things through Christ who strengthens me"*, **Philippians 4:13**. This, to me, is an infomercial of God's power. This is a very tricky scripture to use because, you're showcasing that we can do all things; not some things, big things, small things but **all** things through Christ that gives us strength. Physical strength is not the only thing God was talking about in this passage.

As a soldier in the Army of the Lord, we are going to face many spiritual and mental obstacles; the enemy is constantly trying to stop us from following our leader. Everything in us is going to be tested and giving up will be a regular thought in our mind. If **Philippians 4:13**, however, means something to you then you must decide if you are going to believe the unseen truth or the visible threat that is constantly around you. It's this scripture that we hold on to when we are diagnosed with deadly diseases and we need the strength to hold on while we hope for healing. It's this scripture we hold on to when temptation is knocking at the door and we want to just answer and let it in. **Philippians 4:13** is our reference and go to when we are in need of his guidance and when God's ways are not clear, but He asks us to trust him even though it may seem completely impossible.

There are also many who use this verse as a balance beam when they walk that very thin line of temptation. They think that they can dabble in certain things and when it gets too hard or it goes too far they can suddenly chant this scripture like a magic spell and it all gets better. They use this scripture—and others like it—and mistranslate it's true meaning as an excuse for why they are "bored" at church, or why it's no big deal to ditch church for the sporting events that they adore week after week. After missing 6 to 8 weeks of church—when they see their world falling apart—they resort back to scripture as a source of hope believing that if they just hold on to that all will be made right.

Many who practice their Christianity this way fail to realize that using the Word of God in this manner is like buying a lawn mower but never using it to cut the grass. They see that the grass is getting tall and they take the mower out of the shed because they know that it possess the power to handle the problem; yet they don't use it. Many believers know the scriptures they are supposed to use in their times of trouble and they take them out and quote them against their problems. But the scriptures are not just meant to be *quoted* they are meant to be *lived* out. They are meant to be used as weapons of knowledge and strength.

So I'll ask you the question…

Are you a good advertisement of God's strength and of who He is?

Janelle

Have you ever come across someone who made your struggles seem like nothing because of all they were enduring? Was there ever a time in your life when you knew that if you had half the problems the other person had, you don't think you would survive? Well let me tell you about a young lady by the name of Janelle who was in my youth group years ago. This young lady has been such an inspiration to all those she was around. I have had the pleasure of seeing her greatest prayer request answered.

One evening, while we were conducting youth group, we asked if anyone had any prayer request. Several of the kids asked for things that most fourteen-sixteen year olds would ask for: help in school, help with a test, to win a game they were playing that week. While others were praying for God to help them with their grades, Janelle was praying, "God give me a new heart." She was not asking for her heart to change towards God, but she really needed a brand new beating heart for a transplant, as hers was failing. Her spiritual heart was as tender and as loving as it got, but she was born very physically ill. I know that if every one of those teens just got a piece of her spiritual heart, or her character, it would change them dramatically. Many of them were spoiled in so many ways and their circumstances were minut in comparison to hers.

In Janelle's generation, many of her peers walked away from the Lord for ridiculous reasons. One actually tried to kill himself because he felt that God would not make him good. This young man blamed God for his impulsive behaviors and got mad at God when things did not go his way. He had perfect health and a roof over his head and parents that wanted him to think about the consequences of his actions. This sent him into a tailspin of bad behaviors and he eventually became addicted to drugs and adopted a dangerous and careless lifestyle.

On the other hand you have Janelle who was diagnosed with Leukemia from a very young age. The cancer and the other treatments cause damage to her heart. When I met her she was so small, but she had the biggest personality, not because she was loud, but because all those who knew her situation understood her to be a walking miracle.

I spoke with Janelle's former dean and teacher. I asked both of them how she was in school. I thought that because of her constant admissions to the hospital, her grades must have suffered drastically, but her teacher said, "Her work ethic was amazing. Everything was always on time, books were read and projects were turned in. She never had problems with getting assignments in on time. There were students who slept through my whole class, but when Janelle came, she was always alert and ready to participate. She, if anyone, had an excuse to sleep through my class because of her weak condition, and no one would think anything was wrong with it."

Her dean said that she never got in trouble or caused a problem, still he identified more with her parents. How could a parent handle the constant hospitalization of their child? How does a parent handle their child constantly being on the brink of death from the moment they were born? How would you handle it? I have children and I don't know what I would do if I was always uncertain if my child would live or die from one day to the next.

Her dean went on to say that her parents always seemed so steady, grounded in their faith and spiritually stable. Janelle, as well, seemed always to have faith that was unwavering. He went on to say, "It has always intrigued me in this job that there are people like Janelle who have had such incredible odds, who seem to thrive. They seem to be willing to push against all odds while people who have relatively small issues—by comparison— seem to fall apart. It makes me think of a scripture, *"If you falter in a time of trouble, how small is your strength!" (Proverbs 24:10)*

Before her dean spoke those words and quoted this scripture, he told me of a story of another young man in his school. He was in a total opposite circumstance than Janelle. This young man was from a well-to-do home, but he struggled badly with discipline. His mother was ill and was suffering from arthritis, it was hurting him to see her suffer. One day the young man came into the dean's office and asked, "If God is so wonderful why doesn't he heal my mother?"

After more discussion and probing the dean's response was, "Listen God can do anything, but what you want is to control God. You want God to do what you want, but you don't want to do what God wants. You want God to heal your mother and you want to party every Saturday night at the bar with your friends in West Hampton. That's not how it works. God has given you a free will, you can do whatever you want, but you can't get upset with God if he isn't getting on your program, because that's not how it works."

That is truth and his answer was not only right and just to a rebellious teenager, it is also right for us as well who have been in the faith for a while. Ministers and leaders, do you want to know why some of our churches won't breakout into a revolution that changes the world—it is quite simple—it's because many of our congregations are trying to control God.

This young man was so used to having anything he wanted, whenever he wanted it and he thought that God would follow suit. He always had money, and a big house, and always went on fantastic trips, but it just never occurred to him that he was privileged. He, like us, are upset when God won't allow himself to be controlled. We can't manipulate Him to give us what we want and it's our response to His inability to be controlled in our circumstances, that shows what we are truly made of.

Are you spiritually stable in your faith? Do you sway back and forth with the waves of life? Do you believe God one day, but doubt Him another? What are the circumstances in your life that are causing you to sway so readily? Are you like a tree with deep roots planted by the rivers of living water, or are you like moss on a rock—alive but with no roots—no depth and able to be easily peeled off?

As soldiers for Christ we are supposed to be able to advertise the power of God through the way we live *our* lives. He does not take away our weaknesses, but He strengthens us through our weaknesses. I have learned that I get stronger when I am faced with my own weaknesses. I know that there have been times when I quoted verses just to comfort myself in times of hard seasons. But I also knew that I had to live by those same words and make them a part of my life and choices. The world laughs at some of the examples given by believers today. I'm tired of those Christians who have made their walk all about repeating memorized scripture instead of actually living the life they claim to be holding onto in their hearts.

Here is a little more of that poem from Chapter One.

I am more than a conqueror. I will always triumph.
I can do all things through Christ.
Devils cannot defeat me.
People cannot disillusion me.
Weather cannot weary me.
Sickness cannot stop me.
Battles cannot beat me.
Money cannot buy me.
Governments cannot silence me and hell cannot handle me!
I am a soldier

When we are committed soldiers that understand the power God has given us, we are confident to look our enemies straight in their eyes and promise to overtake them. We are like spiritual Jack Bauers. It doesn't matter the obstacle, the pain, the challenge that is before us, we will be victorious. When our enemy looks at us he laughs because he thinks he has the upper hand. But when we can do all things through God who strengthens us, we won't make idol threats we only make promise.

CHAPTER FIVE

Soldier or Super Hero

Courage is not the absence of fear.
But the will to face it.
- *Anonymous*

As I grew into young adulthood, I needed to humble myself and recognize that I could not fight the enemy the same way I fought the boys in school. The enemy was very different. With the boys in school I could size them up and see either the fear or confidence on their faces. The boys and I shared blows that we could recover from. With the enemy it is not the same.

In the upcoming chapters I am going to talk to you about the enemy we fight. But there are some things I want us to think about together before we get there. Like I told you, I'm not the kind of woman who watches girly sappy flicks. I truly find excitement in playing video games till I have calluses on my fingers. I also enjoy watching movies about superheroes like, The Hulk, Superman, Iron Man, Green Lantern, etc.

Recently, my husband and I popped popcorn, got some soda, put the kids to bed and had two movie nights watching, "The Amazing Spider-Man", and "The Amazing Spider-Man 2", with Andrew Garfield. Sam told me that I would really like them, but I refused—practically boycotted these two films. My reason laid in my loyalty to the Toby McGuire version of Spiderman; so the idea of another Spiderman was ridiculous to me. After watching both movies I truly needed to swallow my pride and admit that I am now an Andrew Garfield fan! (Sorry Toby. I still love you though.) I absolutely loved those movies.

Of all the superheroes though, my favorite is Batman. My Pastor and I completely differ on this topic. He *thinks* Superman is better than Batman—he's totally losing his senses and desperately needs Jesus—because Batman is clearly superior for more reasons than one. Several years ago the Cartoon Network came out with two animated series, one of Batman with Kevin Conroy as the voice (this one came out first I would like to add) and the other was Superman with Tim Daly as the voice. Villain after villain would challenge these two Superheroes. It was in the battles that you would see their weaknesses and witness the close calls of their demise; however the two superheroes refused to depend on each other to help defeat these enemies.

In the Spiderman movies that I watched with my hubby, I found that he was a lot like Batman and Superman in that he relied on no one. His fear of hurting those close to him, led to him taking on the weight of New York City's crimes all by himself. He felt responsible and he spent his time on the walkie talkies helping the police officers catch the bad guys single handedly. I thought that this character must be so lonely because only one other person knew who he really was. He was pushed to the limits physically and had no one else to rely on. The thing he loved doing—helping those in need—was the same thing tormenting him each day. Spiderman constantly had to rely on his makeshift webbing and his own motivational drive to rescue his beloved city from the growing crime.

In watching this I started to ask myself if we, as Christians, have a superhero complex? Have we taken on the mentality that we can handle the blows of life by ourselves? Have we thought that serving the Lord is just like lifting up the hammer of Thor while saying some chant as a bolt of lightning comes and gives us strength? Do we think that because we are not of this world, like Superman, we must hide our Christian identity till someone is in need and then put on the tights, ready to beat the enemy till they are a bloody mess? Or how about Ironman who—in order to protect his heart—puts on a protective suit to hide behind his true inner demons and fears? The truth behind all of this is that we act just like these superheroes sometimes— arrogant, prideful and unrealistic about our limits.

Superhero complex

I will be honest with you and myself; I had—and sometimes still have—a superhero complex. As I grew with God in my older teen years and early twenties, I underestimated the enemy's powers. At the age of nineteen I started the grueling process of planning for my wedding (yes I was only 19). I was bombarded with all the silly things I needed to do to make this a "real wedding." I just wanted the marriage, I cared very little about the wedding and getting dressed up—I know there are some women gasping right now—it's the truth for me. Anyway, one day I put everything to the side and started to daydream about the life God said He had for me. God had spoken to me in Bible College concerning the calling He had on my life. I was so stressed out that I needed to let my mind wander into what I was going to be doing in ministry with Sam.

In my mind I was envisioning myself as a superhero; being able to break the chains of the enemy by just showing up on the scene. I believed life was going to be free of fear, struggles and obstacles. I started declaring war on the enemy and his kingdom as if I was invincible to anything he was going to throw at me. I thought that I could deal with him the same way I dealt with those adolescent boys I battled with in school. Even better, I made sure that Satan knew I was serious as I quoted scripture to really seal my threats as if they were my battle cry.

A few months after I announced to the devil that I would be the one to bring him down, I started getting these really bad migraine headaches, the ones that made me retreat to my room and stay in total darkness. My mom was concerned so she made an appointment for me to see a specialist. They did a number of tests which I was able to tolerate, but there was one test in particular that I did not bounce back from.

On Friday October 31, 1997 Sam and my mom accompanied me to my appointment for a spinal tap to check for spinal meningitis. A spinal tap is a test where they insert a needle in between the bones in your spine, and extract some of the fluid that surrounds your brain and spinal cord. They removed the fluid to test it for different infections. My mom warned me that this was a very painful test and that it would leave me immobile for about twenty-four hours, or even the rest of the weekend. I told her I could not stay home because I was going to minister with Sam at his church in the Bronx, the next day. My mother suggested that I cancel, but I told her that I would not let anything keep me down. I was invincible and I saw myself as unstoppable.

The test was everything my mom said it was going to be, but I was confident that God was going to give me the strength to minister the next day. After the test I felt discomfort, but not the pain my mom insisted I was going to be facing. As they were patching me up, all of a sudden, I felt this evil presence and heard, "I have you right where I want you. You think you're going to do as you feel and come into my territory? Now I will destroy everything you think you're going to use against me." I ignored the voice and got on the bus and headed home with Sam.

Several hours later, I noticed that the pain medication was wearing off and the discomfort was quickly turning into extreme pain. Sam eventually went home while I rested with the hopes of feeling relief when I woke up. I was sadly mistaken. After waking up I was in worse pain than ever before. My head felt like it was going to explode. It was as if my spine had been crushed in the area where the needle was inserted. I could not move a toe or roll over without clenching my teeth in sheer agonizing pain. My mom called from work and I told her what I was going through, she told me this was the reason it was best to cancel my plans for the weekend, so I did just that.

My mom reassured me that the pain would wear off within forty-eight hrs. To our surprise, forty-eight hours came and went and the pain was building dramatically. I was working as a teacher's aide at my church's private school and I didn't want to call out. I still thought I was invincible so I foolishly went to work anyway and pushed passed the pain—that's what superheroes would do right— and showed the enemy who was really in charge. That Monday I woke and got ready for work. The school that I worked for was also the one that Peter, my little brother, was attending. The first hour of walking around wasn't so bad, but as I got closer to the school it felt like I was going to pass out from the pain. When I arrived I needed to lie down because everything was spinning. My legs, my back and hips were on fire. I laid down for twenty minutes before the kids showed up, but it did not help. I was completely crippled with this pain and nothing was taking it away. Within an hour of being at the school I broke down and told my boss I needed to go back home. This was the enemy, I knew it, but I could not get my body to fight the attack that he was raging on it.

I had to make the painful forty five minute travel back home, and this time, by myself. I honestly didn't think I was going to make it home. I stumbled into the house and scrambled desperately for some place to lie down. It felt as if an eighteen wheeler was running over my body with every step. What was going on? Why wasn't this pain going away? I called my mom and she contacted the doctor who said that there was nothing they could do; I just needed to wait it out. I was not worried. It would soon wear off, wouldn't it?

One week later I wasn't better only getting worse by the day. I was unable to sit or stand because the pain caused stars to come to my eyes—I wasn't even able to walk without pain. The only position that gave a bit of comfort was when I was laying down completely still. I was quickly growing impatient and angrier, I remember the words Satan spoke to me one week earlier and I was still unfazed. In pure defiance I spewed out some more vague threats, "This will not keep me down. You have not won. The more you attack me the angrier I'm getting. I promise you when this is all over, I will rage war against you." *But what if it doesn't end,* I thought quietly to myself.

What do you think happened next? Did I rise to my feet and praise God? Did I feel the power of God as an angel came and sprinkled dust on me, making me stronger than I was before? Absolutely not!! Guys I was stupid and arrogant. That day the pain shot up from the middle of my back, and just when I thought that it could not get any worse, it did. A few days after, I woke up completely paralyzed in pain this time from my neck down which shot all the way through my arms. I was even unable to move my neck from side to side, the pain was so excruciating that I could have passed out if I moved the wrong way. This was the moment that I couldn't hold it in anymore. I just wept. I could not believe the amount of pain I was in. The room was spinning so fast, I was unable to even think. I know the enemy was getting a kick out of my breakdown; I could almost hear him laughing.

A humbled rookie

During this time, I only remembered eating once because the pain was too horrific for me to sit up and have a meal—my poor loved ones felt totally helpless.

I was eventually reduced to crawling to the bathroom because I could not stand up. Did Satan finally have me? Was I beat? That's how I felt when my own words were echoing in my head as I was on all fours going to the potty—some superhero. I declared that I was going to go into his kingdom and bring him down but I couldn't even take two steps without screaming for mercy. I made claims that God was going to be by my side as I trampled on the enemy's head, but at that moment the only thing that was trampled was my ego.

Was I a threat to the enemy? Why would he be afraid of me stomping into his kingdom and setting people free when I was reduced to crawling to the bathroom and downright bed bound? I refused to be beat and I was going to show him that I was not your average woman. I was a fighter by nature and I was going to fight the enemy my way. I planned to go to work the next day and that would be the beginning of me overcoming him—so I thought.

I woke up the next morning and things weren't too bad. I was going to command my body to obey *me* not some demon of sickness! I got to the school and started walking up the stairs and the pain hit me again, but I was not going to let it stop me. I would push through this. But my glory was short lived. I was absolutely humiliated as my body began to slowly lock up on me. I felt so weak that I was pleading to lay down on the school mats for relief, once again. My students and boss stood over me while I laid on the floor like someone had knocked me down. That was exactly how I felt, like I was in a fight and got KO-ed.

They called a cab and gave me strict orders not to return to work until I was better. I got in the cab, told the driver where I lived and laid my face on the dirty seat for relief. As I laid there broken in spirit, tears ran down my face—I needed this to go away. Who I was before this whole ordeal, was being stripped away and I didn't see it then but this was a good thing.

My mom called the doctor a third time, this was going on for two weeks and was getting worse fast. He finally prescribed pain medications. Just when I thought things couldn't get worse it sure did. The pain was not as bad but something else was now wrong. I started throwing up violently. I swore that I was going to die because throwing up with this pain in my head and spine was taking me to the top. My mom asked me if she should take me to the hospital, but I refused; that was the sign of defeat, a sign of weakness and I was not going to show that I was weak. We did not realize right away that the medication was causing the vomiting, so I spent days like this.

Everyone around me knew that this attack on me was spiritual and I was too stubborn to show that I was beat. I would not raise my white flag of defeat. I now have four children and two of them were born through C-section. I say this with all honesty, I would rather have them cut me open from side to side without anesthesia, take out my intestines, yank out an 8 lb human, stuff my insides back in random order, and stitch me up again, than have to go through one hour of the pain that I was in that day.

On the third week of this horrible ordeal, my mother asked me if it was okay for her to go to church. I told her to go ahead, while she was away at church, I had a vision that I knew was from the enemy. I saw Sam at the altar and everyone was standing, but I was still sitting. When I looked I was bound to a wheelchair. I heard the enemy say, "This is your fate. You will be going down the aisle in a wheelchair—Sam will never marry you like that. Not only won't you get married, but you will never dance again; you'll be bound to your bed forever. I'm going paralyze you for good, then we'll see if you can do what you threatened."

Tears rolled down the side of my face as they had been for days. All I could say was, "I will not be in a wheelchair. I will dance again. God is in control." In all honesty, I said it, but I did not believe it. I uttered the words out of desperation that it would not lead to that, I was trying to convince myself more than anything, but the enemy was wearing me down. I know that three weeks doesn't sound like a long time, but I can assure you, this was no ordinary experience.

When my mother returned home from church she told me how wonderful the service was. The power of God fell down and a word from the Lord came to one of the ladies in the church who told her, "Everything that Marsha is going through is spiritual warfare, Satan is threatened by her and he is trying to destroy her. She must stand strong. God will bring healing to her body soon." Stand? Why would they use that word? It was the one thing I could not do physically, but I could do it spiritually. I needed to hear that more than she knew.

Unfortunately, this news did not relieve me; it just gave me an anchor to hold on to during this storm of life. A few more days went by and it was clear that I was very allergic to the medicine they had prescribed which caused me to vomit so violently. I was still in pain when I was on it, but I was able to walk around a little longer and sit up to eat. Once I was off the medication I was reduced to crawling to get around again. My mom couldn't take it any longer and almost one month later she made an appointment with a neurologist.

The neurologist checked me and said after a spinal tap the body is supposed to start closing up the hole made by the needle. In my case that's not what happened. The needle left an open hole causing the fluid in my spine to leak out. The fluid is what keeps the brain afloat so when we walk around the brain will not rub or bang against the skull. When I was laying down the fluid would build up a little, but once I sat up it would leak out and my movements caused my brain to hit against my skull. The fix was simple, they just needed to put ***another*** needle in my back and inject my blood to seal the original hole. That was not happening, I thought, but I could not live like this one more day. We made the appointment and went back home.

I retreated to my room and closed the door. I cried a little more at the idea of another needle going into my spine. Fear gripped me and I called out to God. I needed Him more than ever. Before I got sick I was working on dancing to a song by Fred Hammond called, "Promise Keeper." I was so desperate to dance because I could not get over the idea that I would have to let this doctor put a needle in my back again. I turned on my stereo and played the song. I was not in much pain surprisingly, and I knew I had a few minutes before I would start feeling it again so I decided to use that time to finish the song. I started dancing which turned into worship. I had never been so desperate for healing in all my life. I sang the words of this song like my life depended on it with a few moves.

Seasons come and then they go,
But all you have established shall hold fast
And on that we can rest assure.
And beyond imagination,
Every promise you have given me will come true.

I see you, so sovereign
You are the only God so wise.
In your hands you hold my times.
I can hold you to your word.
You're never wavering, you won't turn.
For I am sure, that you are the Promise Keeper.

Exceeding all my expectations,
I find myself believing you
With no hesitation.
Cause you prove to me you're awesome,
I can clearly see my life is yours, El-Shaddai.

Heaven and earth will pass away before one word you
speak will ever pass away.

By the end of the song, I was still pain free. I went in my mom's room and started watching T.V. with her, twenty minutes went by and I was still fine. She was amazed that I was able to sit up so she brought me a plate of food and I was able to eat the whole meal without having to lie down in between. I was feeling pressure on my back, but nothing like I had been feeling for almost a month. To my surprise, which shouldn't have been a surprise, God healed me after that dance.

That season I had learned a very humbling lesson, I was not a superhero able to spew out whatever I wanted. I was a soldier who needed to learn about waiting for my orders from my Commanding Officer. I walked into the enemy's territory and told him everything I was going to do. I took up a responsibility that God did not place on me. He attacked me. Satan does not waste his time on talkers; his time is too short for that. But when a threat is raised, he must destroy it before it becomes something dangerous. My issue was that I underestimated my enemy and overestimated my ability—those are the perfect ingredients for failure.

Elijah, the Bible version of Thor

One of the reasons I love Batman more than Superman is that he has no superpowers. He is not from another planet, he doesn't call on his gods for help, he doesn't have a lantern to give him strength; he is just a very strong and determined human being. Bruce Wayne's (Batman without the mask) hate for crime was stemmed from the death of his father and mother who were murdered in an alley by a thief when he was just a boy. Once Bruce grew up he promised himself he would not just sit back while these crimes took place and other people were hurt. It was his hate for evil that drove his determination to rid the city of the villains and criminals that were gaining strength every day in Gotham. The only issue I have with my dark knight is he would rather do it all alone. He never liked calling out for help. He felt he was the only one that could do the job. Batman kept all of his relationships and friends to a minimal because he wanted to live his life alone. He felt that it was better if he didn't need to worry or depend on anyone.

Let's talk about Elijah in the Bible; he would definitely be a superhero if he were alive today. He was able to stop his land from getting rain for 3 ½ years (*1 Kings 17 : 18*). In the meantime he was fed by scavenging birds and he made food appear out of nowhere for him, a widow, and her son. He also raised people from the dead and there was even a show down of the gods featuring Baal and the Almighty Elohim— the Lord won, hands down, no contest, burning up everything including rocks! Elijah went on to slaughter 450 of the prophets that worshiped Baal all by himself!! Did you read that? Stop and think about that before you move on, this man killed the equivalent of some church's attendance, times three; one by one he killed 450 people. He seems to be unstoppable and emotionless.

After this incident there was another encounter that Elijah had which I have never heard any pastor preach about yet. The story is found in *2 Kings 1*. There was a king that was out to seize Elijah, and so he sent fifty soldiers out to get him. When the captain saw Elijah, he called out to him and said, "O Holy Man! Come down right now!" Elijah's response is out of this world… "If it's true that I am a 'holy man,' lightning strike you and your fifty men."

Guess what happened, blue lightning came down and killed the men just as he said. The arrogant king sent another group of fifty men to get Elijah and guess what happened? You're right; he did the exact same thing to those men. What kind of man has the divine protection of God like this? The king sent another group of fifty, but the last group of men were different and came with more reverence so the Lord told Elijah he could go with them with no fear.

Man, reading something like this you would think Elijah lived his life fearless, unstoppable, and almost invincible, to me, he was Thor and Batman put together. Unfortunately, between killing four hundred and fifty prophets of Baal and striking hundred men with lightning he was in a cave in 1 Kings 19 crying like a pansy because *one woman*, Jezebel, threatened to kill him. His reason for fear and cowardice behavior was because he felt no one else in the whole world loved God but him. Come on Elijah? Really? I suppose I can't be that judgmental because aren't we like that at times? Don't we have a pity party when everything around us is crumbling?

Well anyway, she must have been a big woman with shaven teeth, eyes of fire, with a belt around her waist initialed BK for Butt Kicker. It makes no sense why a man who had the ear of God Almighty, who did almost anything for him, (like changing the weather forecast for three and a half years), would run because one mere woman challenged him. He became suicidal just because she told him that she would do the same to him as he did to her prophets. He asked God to take his life; he was ready to meet his ancestors. Wow, this was the same man displaying the power of God by one prayer.

Elijah fled and slept under a tree. God woke him up and fed him. Elijah used the strength of that food to continue running for another forty days just to go to a cave. What blows my mind is when God speaks to him; he asked this question to Elijah, "Why are you here?" That is the worst question God could ask one of His own children. Elijah was so scared that he had left the path God had for him. I don't know if any of you have ever had that moment—when you are so full of fear and doubt because of the challenges before you—that not even God knows why you are where you are. How many times do we overestimate our strength and underestimate God's abilities? How many times do we let the fear of the battle scare us more than the actual battle? Fear of our enemy should never put us on a path that not even God knows why we're there.

Sometimes we forget a lot of things in the battle we're in.

> *12 For our struggle is not against flesh and blood, but against the rulers, against the authorities, against the powers of this dark world and against the spiritual forces of evil in the heavenly realms.* **Ephesians 6:12**

Look at the verse again; we are not fighting humans, what does that mean to us? Well that means that if we are being challenged by a human being, it's not that person we need to focus on, but the spiritual part of it. We have to stop focusing on each other and start seeking God for wisdom on how to deal with the matter.

The scripture goes on to say what we do battle against:

1. *The rulers*
2. *The authorities*
3. *The powers of this dark world and*
4. *The spiritual forces of evil in the heavenly realm.*

When I challenged the enemy I was unaware of whom I was fighting. My cockiness and arrogance stirred up the hornet's nest. Elijah may not have been sick like I was sick, but he and I had a lot in common with arrogance and pride. He slaughtered four hundred and fifty all by himself, but kept his eyes on one woman. What went wrong? Let's look at where this all began, look at *1 Kings 18:1-2.*

> *¹After many days, the word of the Lord came to Elijah in the third year, saying, go, <u>show yourself</u> to Ahab, and I will send rain upon the earth.*
> *² So Elijah went to present himself to Ahab.*

God's instruction to Elijah was to just **show himself to Ahab** because God wanted to bring rain back to Israel. Look at what Elijah does instead

> *"When Ahab saw Elijah, Ahab said to him, Are you he who troubles Israel? ¹⁸ Elijah replied, I have not troubled Israel, but you have, and your father's house, by forsaking the commandments of the Lord and by following the Baals. ¹⁹ Therefore send and gather to me*

*all Israel at Mount Carmel, and the 450 prophets of
Baal and the 400 prophets of [the goddess] Asherah,
who eat at [Queen] Jezebel's table.* (**Verse 17-19**)

Elijah gets upset and it's here that he challenges the four
hundred and fifty prophets of Baal to a show down. He was
tired of them disrespecting the God he loved and served, so he
felt it was time to defend God's honor. That was not what God
told him to do. He was only suppose to show himself to Ahab
and God would bring the rain. One thing I learned early in
my walk with God is, if I were going to threaten the enemy, I
needed to make sure that I was able to handle what was going
to take place *after*. I never ever cower down to the enemy. What
I have learned to do though is to stop making idle threats to
the enemy. I need to make promises, **promises I can keep**.
I have to make declarations and learn that before I speak to
the enemy, I need to search for the leading of the Holy Spirit
and find scriptures to confirm my authority and then I need to
make a promise to give Satan the fight of his life, then deliver.

Elijah was successful at beating Baal, because God knew
He was all powerful, but Elijah had mistaken God's power for
his own. We must not mistake our own finite powers with the
powers of the Almighty One. We also must not think that we
can manipulate God to do what we want. We are not the ones
who give the orders. We cannot forget that God knows our
heart **and** our motives. If we want to defeat the enemy just
to feed our egos then we will fall. God will not play a part in
making us think more highly of ourselves than we ought to.
God needs us to have the heart of a soldier not the ego of a
superhero.

CHAPTER SIX

The Heart of a Soldier

Out of suffering have emerged the strongest souls; the most massive character are seared with scars.
- Kahlil Gibran

Where it all began...

At some point in my life I found myself looking for God to show me the next step. I wanted to know what God had in store for me. I was in need of answers to where I was going with my life. In my late teens in Bible College many felt called to go to places like China and Africa, but I found myself just simply not knowing what I was going to do with my life. I knew that I was where He wanted me to be, but what was I doing it for?

One day during my time of prayer the Lord dropped a thought in my spirit, "Others may have a heart for one place for ministry, while you feel that you have no direction. That's because I don't have just one place for you to go, I am going to use you in many places and I don't want one location to be your goal. I am going to use you all over." My heart started racing so hard that it felt as if it was coming out of my chest, but God was not finished speaking with me yet. "I am going to use your testimony to restore the faith of the abused, the rejected, those suffering from depression and those considering suicide. You will minister to many. There are many out there just like you who need to hear your testimony in order to understand how they can get out of where they are." At the time, I could not see how I was in any shape to help anyone, but I believed Him; I knew deep down that He was going to do it. I wanted to see Him fulfill His promise. I **needed** Him to fulfill His promise to me. I also knew that I could not do what He called me to do if I stayed where I was. I needed to follow the proverbial "Yellow Brick Road."

One year after that experience, in 1998, Sam and I went to a Youth Convention in Syracuse New York. We were months away from getting married and life was getting real. The very last day of the convention there was an altar call for those who knew they were called to ministry. Sam and I responded to that call, along with many others, and went up to the altar in obedience and acceptance of God's call for us. As we stood there praying with the expectation of an encounter with God; something supernatural happened to Sam that he has not forgotten to this day. At the altar God fast forwarded Sam's mind to the future but not to a set point in time. What he saw was a time stream—almost like when they go to warp speed in Star Trek—as he was going though it God showed him face after face of teenagers. He felt God say that these were the faces of the young people we would be ministering to.

The faces just kept coming and Sam's emotions kept getting stronger, so strong that he fell to his knees and started weeping. This man was not a crier (and still is not) so this was completely foreign to me. When he retells the story he explains that by the time he hit the floor his mind was asking "What's going on?" He realized that he had no control over his muscles to stand up and it almost scared him when he realized that he couldn't open his eyes. The faces kept coming and zooming past him. When he finally got up, he was a changed man. He heard the calling of the Lord before. A woman prophesied to him, when he was fourteen years old; to minister to young people, but Sam had hopes in other areas. Now he was ready to face his calling.

Jesse

Fast forward two years later, Sam became the youth pastor of his home church and I was right there with him. Though he was the Youth Pastor we worked together in the ministry. It was where I needed to be. It's how we have always seen it and how it remains to this day. A few months into this new role as youth leaders a girl named Jessie came into our youth group. She was only twelve years old, but Jesse was one of the shortest little firecrackers I would ever meet. She was completely "thugged out", with her bandana, big clothes and no-nonsense attitude. Jesse sat in our youth services every Sunday and barely said a word. As she kept coming it became clear that she was doing so with the intent to find answers. When I finally got her to open up a bit, I was shocked to find out that she had been coming to our church all by herself.

"You're here by yourself?" I marveled, "How did you start coming here?"

"Well I was on the bus and I saw the church. I thought this was a catholic church so I decided to check it out."

"Your mom just let you come?" I asked confused.

"Yeah," she replied like that was the most natural thing.

I decided to take some more time and get to know this girl a bit more because everything about her intrigued me. Her home life was a complete mess, her self-esteem was as low as it could be and her concept of God was warped and corrupt. Our youth group seemed to have something she wanted, but she was not ready to let go of her fears and doubts just yet. Jesse felt that this "God thing" was good for us, but it wasn't for her. She called us "Holy Rollers" and "Goody two-shoes."

Jesse would refuse to show emotion during the worship times and found crying as a sign of pure weakness. She had the heart of a fighter, but she didn't realize that she was fighting the wrong thing, as I did when I was younger. The more she came to the youth group, the more her exterior walls came down. She started to love us and loved being part of the group but she still kept the wall she had built around her heart very guarded.

Every week, God chipped at that wall so that she could find trust and protection in Him. I knew the importance of investing in my young people during that stage of their life because my youth pastor did the same for me. My pastor was a loving, upfront, strong, faithful spiritual father to me and Jesse was a life that I felt God calling me to in the same way. She eventually gave her life to the Lord, but the road to Jessie's trust was not over. As I grew closer to her I understood that winning Jesse's heart was going to be hard and that once I had it I would be holding on to something very precious and not easily obtained.

Her relationship with her parents was not ideal and her perspective on life was worse. She wanted to believe that God was good, but she had a huge problem with seeing Him as the "Good Father." Her example of a father was not one of hope but of abandonment. Not too long after we met her, Jessie had found out the man whom she believed was her father, really wasn't. When she found out the truth of her father it made her close up and not trust people. Now God wanted to be a "Father" to her? The concept didn't sit well with Jesse. I used our times together to tell her about my relationship with my father and of how I had to believe my relationship with God was something different. I showed her my spiritual scars and felt okay with doing so anytime she needed me to. I made myself vulnerable to her because I saw myself in her eyes.

One day God and Jesse had a wrestling match of sorts and thankfully Jesse lost. We had just finished having a very powerful youth service and the power of God fell strongly on the youth. Many of them were crying and praying at the altar, Jesse included. I went over to her and she started rocking side to side; I asked her what was going on and she said that she felt like crying, but she couldn't bring herself to do it.

Jesse was broken because of the things that had happened to her in her family. Her mother was verbally abusive to her and her other sibling and throughout the years she had lied to her about many things which left her scratching for the truth. She found out that not only did her father abandon her but he started another family. Jesse held on to her anger towards her family for many years and God wanted to help carry her, to relieve her from the weight however she was too scared to let it go. This was what had been preventing her from trusting people and what she used to protect herself from getting hurt. If she could not trust her own family what made Sam and I and the other leaders, who cared for her, worthy of her trust? How could she believe in this God that we were all talking to her about? To cry and let God in required her to become vulnerable and admit she was hurt, angry and scared. All of those things she felt and believed were signs of weakness.

Jesse was so hurt by the things she had gone through that she did not want to pray for her unsaved family, she was actually afraid that they *would* get saved. She was so hurt that she knew praying for their salvation would mean that they could escape hell. Jesse wanted them to go to hell. But God wanted this angry young girl—with a heart of stone—to be made new and find release from her hurt. She wrestled with God for sometime at that altar, but finally she broke.

My heart bled for hers because the wrestling she was doing was so obvious. I softly whispered in her ear, "Jesse just let go." It was like watching someone hanging off of a cliff, God is at the bottom telling them to let go—He'll catch them—but they are too afraid. Her grip was slipping at that moment; Jesse looked me in the eyes and stared for a moment. I could see it happen as she closed her eyes again and the first tear started running down her face. The love of God flooded over her in such a major way, you could see the hand of God peeling away her grip on her own heart.

God began a work in her that was not to be reversed. She cried like she had never cried before. Jesse could not hold it back any longer. I put my arms around her and held her as she wept for everything she had been through. With her arms wrapped around me, she gripped my shirt like someone who was in agonizing pain; all I could do was be there, be the person who held her through her breakthrough. Her clinched fist eventually opened and the power of God continued to work. Her emotions brought her to the floor as the music played that night.

Jesse's journey after that day changed her into a brand new person. She was one of the most compassionate, loving people I came to know with a heart of flesh and not of stone. She held that rough exterior for a while, but when the power of God moved she was not capable of resisting it. Her boldness for God grew day by day. She spoke of God in her home and soon everyone in her home came to church regularly. They eventually gave their hearts to the Lord and she was baptized shortly after her breakthrough. Jessie didn't stop there; she spoke of God in her school and was willing to take on the administration when she started bringing her Bible to school. She took every opportunity to talk about God even in her math class. How can she talk about God and math you ask? Well that girl actually told her math teacher that Jesus *multiplied* the loaves and fishes. She became the "Holy Roller" and "Jesus Freak."

Jesse's love for God was evident to her peers in everything that she did. She witnessed to her friends and brought many of them to youth group. Her influence was so great in school she got our youth dance team to minister at a special event. One big accomplishment was when she spoke to her principal about God. She invited her to one of the shows that we were holding. Jesse didn't think she would ever see her in our church, but to her surprise her principal was in the audience taking it all in. Jesse was one of the most powerful teens in that youth group and I will always remember her and how she inspired Sam and myself to never doubt the power of God.

Carlee

On August 6, 2006 Sam and I moved to our current church where there awaited for us a wonderful group of teens who needed a new youth leader. They had been without a real youth pastor for almost two years. The group from our previous church was so much different from this new group. The group from before was located in the Bronx and their issues were much more serious and, in some cases, even life threatening. Those kids were hardcore, they could be considered sometimes (almost all the time) challenging and intense. The kids in our new church were low key and the issues were not as threatening as those from the Bronx.

Four or five years into our time of serving in our new church we met a young lady by the name of Carlee who was just turning twelve. Carlee, on the outside seemed like all the other clueless pre-teens in the church. Many times I would see her with her friends and ask her when she was coming to youth group. She made up all these lame excuses as to why she did not come and made false promises about coming to the future meetings. Time went on and Carlee came about one or two times, but it was clear she had no interest in really joining the group. She just wanted to get me off her back; to her annoyance, I did not leave her alone.

There were times when I, jokingly, threatened her and we both laughed about it, but I really felt that she needed to be a part of the youth group. There was something about her that was pushing me not to give up and I didn't really know why I felt so strongly about her.

A year or so later I was in a women's meeting at church and her mother was there as well. When the time for sharing came, her mother opened up to all of us about Carlee who was now thirteen. Her mother was at her wits end with her daughter—after finding out that she had been lying to her about her whereabouts. Carlee was caught in a string of lies and her mother discovered that she had been meeting up with her boyfriend at the movies.

Life got very complicated for this teen so I took the opportunity to speak with her mother after the women's meeting. I pulled her to the side and got a little more information about what took place. Her mother was desperate so I asked her about bringing Carlee to youth group whether she liked it or not. After a few weeks of being forced to go, Carlee came to enjoy being at youth group. Even though she embraced the group it was obvious to me that she had yet to accept a relationship with God.

Over the years, I watched this young girl change, but in a weird way. With her mouth she spoke of God's love and his grace, but with her actions she did another. Something was going on and I wasn't too sure what that was. At the age of seventeen, Carlee went into a dangerous direction. God spoke to me and told me that Carlee was suicidal. There was no outside evidence of this and I questioned the voice I heard. Still unsure, I started talking to Carlee and after a while she admitted that she had had quick thoughts of suicide, but nothing serious. Something was seriously wrong with her, but I was not able to put a finger on it. Within a month of our conversation, Carlee's thoughts of suicide became real and she was soon admitted into a hospital under surveillance.

Sam and I knew we needed to intervene in some way because her mother was at the end of her rope and did not know what else to do. It was so uncomfortable to be sitting in a hospital waiting for them to bring her out. When they finally brought her out, our hearts were so tender to her because it was visible that she was broken in so many ways, physically, mentally, emotionally, and spiritually. As we sat with her, she shared that she finally admitted to her mother, and the hospital, that she was living with the pain of being secretly abused by her father physically, verbally and sexually; from the age of three years old to nine years old.

Several memories of her past, for some reason, resurfaced to her mind and she didn't know what to do with them. She remembered after her parents divorced that when she went to stay with her father he would severely abuse her—mostly at night. At that time her mother was trying to get her life right with God and sharing it with her. Carlee's mother told her how this invisible being, in a place called Heaven, would protect her and help her whenever she needed Him. Carlee started praying to this God to save her at night from the abuse and at times she was spared because her father was too drunk. But at other times she had to endure nights of pain and agony. It was here that her doubts about this God began. As she got older and was being told about her Heavenly Father, bitterness and anger started to consume her. How could she receive God as a "Good Father" when she felt that her earthly father was the epitome of evil? What kind of loving God would give her such a brutal life?

Over the course of time Carlee was molested and verbally abused by the different men. The trauma caused by these men—some long-term some short—caused emotional damage within Carlee. Her body started breaking down as she began to get so physically ill that the doctors didn't know how she was still making it. She grew even sicker by the time she turned seventeen. Finally, the doctors put it together that her home life was posing a threat to her well-being. They broke the news to her mother that Carlee's next physical episode would most likely kill her. It was then that they sent CPS to her home for investigation.

In the six years of ministering to Carlee she had never heard my story of darkness and hopelessness. In the hospital I started sharing with her just a small part of my past, even the part where I wanted to commit suicide. She could not believe it. For so long she felt that there was no way out of her own hurt. Carlee was ashamed of her thoughts and the struggles she was secretly battling, but when she found someone else that battled with the same issues as she, hope ignited in her heart and the fighter in her really came out.

When I left Carlee she made a declaration to herself and to the enemy that she was going to come out of this on top, she was not going to let her past define who she was any longer. Not only was she going to win this battle, but she was also going to help others who were fighting the same war. In the following years I watched Carlee discover who she really was, not the distorted version of herself the enemy had planted in her mind, but she believed that God had a ministry for her in music and with young people.

Can I tell you the truth, my beloved Carlee fell many times after that day? But what I love about her is that she got up more times than the enemy could knock her down. I cried with her as I watched her scratch at the walls for a victory even though it looked like she was defeated. She refused to give up! What kept her fighting? What kept her going? It wasn't my words, the words of the preacher or her mother's words. It was the calling God revealed to her that she was going to minister to others. The faces of those she was going to help became more important than the current pain she was going through.

Carlee is still in a place of struggle as her severe abuse has left her clinging to God to get her through her day and she is fine with that. She has accepted the truth that if she takes her eyes off God for even a second that she will find herself at the edge of death as she was before physically and spiritually. God became the air in her lungs, the ground she walks on, the sight in her eyes and the strength in her spine.

Carlee is pursuing her degree in psychology so she can help other kids that were in her shoes. She has such a tenderness towards those who have gone through kind of darkness. I want to say that Carlee is right where she needs to be but the fighter in Carlee is still fighting. She is still wrestling with her demons. Her God will never let her go no matter what.

Not every fighter sees victory right away. Some battles last longer than others. The length of the battle does not dictate the outcome, our God is capable of walking us through it all.

Do you relate to either of these life experiences? Is there something in your life that God wants to put His hands on but you refuse to let Him? Is there someone who has tainted the character of God in your eyes because of how they have treated you? Well God can use the things that should have destroyed you to strengthen the fighter in you. You may have to fight for what He has for you, but He will take the journey with you.

Carlee and Jesse know what it is like to be overlooked, underestimated, and ignored. God created in them hearts that could endure but the choice to do so was solely on their shoulders. They had to choose to let go of the pain of rejection and hurt. They refuse to give their past the power to control their future.

There is a man whose life is recorded in the Bible—that for us as readers—is a perfect example of a fighter. He was able to defeat giants in his life, physically and spiritually. He is given the title of "A man after God's own heart" and was one of the greatest kings of all time. This man's name was David son of Jesse and he was a Soldier of God. We will learn more about him in the upcoming chapters.

CHAPTER SEVEN

The Soldier With Heart

"One doesn't become a soldier in a week – it takes training, study and discipline."
-Daniel Inouye

I believe that one of the most awesome squad of soldiers ever produced was from Israel during the reign of David. Under David's leadership a group of men/warriors conquered nation after nation who tried to oppose Israel. These men were loyal to David, some calling him their king before he was officially crowned as such. They risked their lives and protected him believing he was truly the anointed man of God. These men loved David and they honored and valued him because of his leadership and his devotion to God.

Among these soldiers were men who were amazing in battle and who were skilled in various forms of combat. A handful of them became legendary warriors showing skill and courage. Some of their stories can be found in the Bible in the book of 2 Samuel, the 23rd chapter.

Before the people of Israel were led by kings, they were held together by the powerful Almighty God. God protected and provided for them through harsh circumstances that, left on their own, would have naturally destroyed them. For many years God used leaders like Moses, Joshua, Deborah, Samson, Samuel, and others (who are recorded in the book of Judges) to help keep—and many times put—Israel on the straight and narrow. Eventually the people of Israel became tired of the wickedness of those who were leading them and demanded to be led by a king. Even though God was not in agreement with their desire for a king, He gave them one anyway.

It is at this moment that we first meet Saul. The Bible says he was tall and impressive. In other words, he was exactly what the people wanted to intimidate their enemies. For awhile this worked out well. Saul's reign began strong and he brought victories to the nation. His heart though, was not to please God first and this began the fall of his kingdom. His first lack of judgment fell upon him when he began to care more about the words of the people over what God had told him. Time and again, Saul would do as he felt was best to appease his critics and followers. And time and again he would go against the laws and commands of God. Eventually, God rejects Saul as king over Israel and has a prophet, Samuel, appoint his successor.

A sixteen year old was the person God felt was the best to take on this immense responsibility. This teenager, David, is not chosen because he will be a flawless king, but because— despite the many wrong mistakes and failures he will embark on —his heart never turns away from God. David, son of Jesse, became the standard that God held all kings and leaders to that followed after. There was about forty two kings and one queen that ruled over Israel in all. Though there were good ones in the bunch, none met up to the level of David's leadership and achievements. Even David's son Solomon—who was wise and helped to make Israel one of the most powerful and riches kingdoms at that time—did not match the character and heart of his father that pleased God.

The more I learned to love the Lord, the more I grew totally absorbed in pleasing God. I wanted to know His heart and how I could grow closer to being what He desired of me. So it made sense to me to follow the steps David made since he had the heart after God's. It was the apostle Paul, in the book of Acts, that expressed God's feelings about King David saying:

> *"After removing Saul, he made David their king. He testified concerning him: 'I have found David son of Jesse, a man after my own heart; he will do everything I want him to do.'"* **Acts 13:22**

I wanted to know how I could get that kind of heart, how I could get God to see me at David's standard? This is what I learned over the years as God changed me.

1. Real soldiers are often underestimated

1 Samuel 16 records God's search for Saul's successor. The Lord has the prophet go out to seek, in the house of Jesse, the one who would become the new king. Jesse had eight sons and Samuel was to anoint one of them to be king. When Jesse's first son, Eliab, came before Samuel his good looks, height and all around soldier like qualities, made Samuel believe that this was the guy who would change Israel. Eliab was surely the one who God has chosen to be the next king, Samuel thought.

Now you have to understand, Samuel had never moved and operated as a prophet without the direction of the Lord. As a little boy, Samuel learned how to hear God's voice and direction. As best we know, never has he confused God's words or intentions, **till this very day**. God speaks to Samuel immediately and tells him, *"You look on the outward appearance but I look on the heart."* It's possible that Samuel was at a stage of "mentally mourning" the loss of Saul that he was trying to replace the current broken king with someone who had the same brokenness. So, looking at Eliab with all his natural qualities, sure he would be a great replacement.

God, however, was not going to pick the new king the same way Saul was picked; knowing that no man would be perfect and sinless. What God sought after was one who would at least have the heart to serve Him.

We are no different then Samuel. How many times do we look at the outward works of a person to determine how qualified they are? I have watched many "talented" people sing on worship teams, teach bible classes or preach a good word, do so without possessing an **anointing**. For me, I'll take the anointing of God over mere talent, any day. I've witnessed churches place talent as a priority and mislead their flock into thinking that the "better" singer and preacher were anointed. How many times do we overlook the one who seems less talented because we won't invest in what is required to help the unqualified be qualified. It is the reason why there are so many sitting in the pews holding on to their gifts and frustrated because they have no outlet to operate. Unfortunately, some leaderships believes that those in the pews are not as good because they are going off of appearance and not the heart. Like Samuel, these leaders do love God but are confused by the word of God. This is when we become people who forfeit character for ability. The outward begins to be what matters most to us and we forget it is in the foundation we find strength, true anointing, heart, devotion and love. What we see on the surface can be faked, falsified, even duplicated but integrity, character and heart is uniquely designed and anointed by God.

Eliab was the first born so it was assumed that he was the greatest, but God likes to shake things up at times and prove that the first shall be last and the last shall be first. He uses things that appear foolish to this world to confuse the wise. Things like taking a little boys lunch—a couple loaves of bread and a few fish—to feed a multitude of people with plenty of leftovers remaining.

Time and again God defies what we know as "logic" just so that we can see His power. By doing so we begin to learn that His ways are not our ways. If there are those who call you unqualified, incompetent and even foolish, then guess what, you may be exactly what God is looking for.

As I walked with God I often looked at my own insecurities and brokenness and—with all that I saw—my conclusion was that I had nothing to offer God. What could I possibly offer to Him that would help the Kingdom? In time though, I noticed something. The Lord blessed me with key people throughout my years that I connected with for moral and spiritual support.

As I reflected one day on how far God has brought me and who He was, I noticed that those individuals were people who were overlooked and/or underestimated over years as well.

I realized that I found it easy to connect with them because they were the runt of the litter, the underdogs and the last to be picked to be on a team. God allowed people who could connect with me and share in my perspective, to be pillars of strength and encouragement. In fact when I thought about it deeper, I realized that I also connected better with the people of the bible who were underdogs as well. The more I read of their situations and circumstances, and how God brought them through, the better I felt about myself and confident that I had a chance.

No offense to others who came into this world talented, strong and accomplished, but those testimonies are harder for me to relate to—as maybe mine may be hard for you to relate to. It was with the trials and obstacles that Simon Peter, James and John dealt in the Bible that I found common ground. They were plain, unlearned fishermen who didn't let their past keep them from the future God had for them. It was the struggles of people like Esther in the Bible—a poor orphan who was forced into the palace and later saved the lives of her people—who inspired me to see that God has a plan even in situations I may not understand. Stories such as these make me feel like I am a prime candidate for an extraordinary life.

2. Real soldiers come in all shapes and sizes

When Samuel was corrected, God told him that Eliab was not the one He had chosen to be the next king of Israel. Samuel then needed to see all the other sons, but none of them were fit to be king either. You can almost tell when reading it that Samuel is a little disappointed when he asks Jesse if these were all the sons he had. In the Message Bible, Jesse tells Samuel that there is one more, "the runt" but he was tending the sheep (*1 Samuel 16:11*). This very statement says a lot.

I think that it is very interesting that Jesse never thought to change places with David—or maybe send one of the rejected sons to tend the sheep—so he could get a chance to be brought before Samuel. It seems as if he had ruled David out because he had no faith in his "runt" of a son—*but God did!!* Whatever the reason is, Jessie didn't consider David. He ruled him out of the equation. Have you ever felt underestimated because of size, intelligence, or financial status?

Samuel waited for someone to replace David at his post so he could be anointed king. He refused to sit until David was brought in and who knows how far he was tending the sheep—trust me it wasn't in the backyard. It could have been miles and miles away. But when Samuel saw David, he knew immediately that he was the teenager for the job. What were the brothers thinking as they watched the most powerful prophet of the time, anoint the smallest and youngest of the clan? I wonder if any of them thought that he had made another mistake like he did in anointing the rejected Saul.

I will not get into it too much in regards to my early life experiences with my father here because my first book, *The Threshing: A Weapon Forged by Fire* discussed that in great detail. But if you have not read it, let me just say that I did not have a father who thought much of me when I was younger. As a result I was so out of control and violent that very little good was expected of me. One of the worst feelings a child can experience is when your own parent has no confidence in you. For a young mind, if you can't rely on your parent's to believe in you, then who can you rely on? If they aren't bringing you before the prophet's face then who else will?

Do not underestimate yourself—or anyone for that matter—because of size or lack of talent. It's sometimes the smallest member of the team that could make the most impact and perform the winning shot. Sometimes it's the thinnest football player who makes the most touchdowns, and it's even the softest singer at times who is chosen to lead the church in worship. I have learned that if God doesn't rule you out, then you have the same chances as anyone else, no matter what your weakness is.

3. Real Soldiers Know Who Is In Charge

Sometime after David had been anointed king, in *I Samuel 17,* a war broke out between the Philistines and the Israelites and his brothers went out to be soldiers in the war. This was not like any other war Israel had faced before. The Philistines had made a simple demand to make this war end nice and simple. They challenged Israel to send out their best warrior and he would fight their best warrior. Winner takes all and there would be no unnecessary bloodshed. Sounds simple enough right? There was one big problem though. The warrior for the Philistines was the nine foot tall champion, Goliath.

Well Israel had Eliab, the great first born of Jesse and Jonathan, the skillful soldier and son of King Saul. Surely one of these great men would step up, but neither of them did. Saul, the mighty king who himself had slain many men and brought about many victories for Israel, surely he would raise up his sword against Goliath before allowing his nation to fall into the hands of the Philistines, but he didn't. To make matters worse, Goliath was taunting the Israelites for forty days demanding for them to send someone man enough to fight him. He hurled insults at them and mocked the God they served. No one had enough guts to challenge him except one person—a wimpy, runty, smelly teenage shepherd boy, name David.

David was obeying his father's wishes and was bringing food to his brothers when Goliath came out across the valley to shout out his daily threat. David, hearing the insults spewing out of the enemy's mouth, turned to the soldiers and asked why they were allowing this Philistine to insult the name of God. Eliab, seeing his little brother questioning the events taking place, accused David of just wanting to be amongst the war. Eliab scolded David and made him seem small by telling him that he needed to get back home to take care of his few sheep. Eliab may have appeared to be the right choice for king, but his heart was surely not of one.

David must have been used to insults because he never even addressed Eliab's comments. Instead he was more appalled that everyone was just standing there doing nothing while this bully of a Philistine was talking about his God in such a disrespectful manner. It's here where we first see what it was that God saw in David that made him the prime choice of being king. If no one else was going to stand up to Goliath, then he volunteered himself to be Israel's champion.

This blasphemer could not be allowed to stand. It angered David that his Lord, his God, was being spoken of that way. David was ready to defend his God's honor. I find it interesting that David didn't care what others said about him, but mess with his God and insult his God's name? Now you have a problem!

After some other formalities David is brought before the king and with complete confidence; David convinced Saul to give him the responsibility of facing Goliath. Scripture tells us that David strategically picked up five smooth stones as ammunition. Armed with his sling—which he has used most likely before to protect his sheep from predators—he stepped up to the battle line. Look at what the enemy says,

> *"Am I a dog that you come after me with a stick?*
> *Come on, I'll make road kill of you for the buzzards.*
> *I'll turn you into a tasty morsel for the field mice."*
> **I Samuel 17:43 MSG.**

The enemy laughed and looked at David's size and thought that this was a joke. Goliath was insulted that this was the one Israel had picked to fight him. But what Goliath didn't know was that this was not just some boy picked off the streets. You see, the way that David spoke about God showed that he had spent many hours praying and worshiping Him. The way in which David was angered about how God was mocked indicated that he not only loved God, he passionately revered Him.

God didn't just tell Samuel to find some kid and anoint him king. He had Samuel go out to find the one that God himself had spent time with and developed a strong relationship with. David knew what it was to be in God's presence. He even told Saul that God delivered him on separate occasions from the hands of a bear and a lion when they came to attack his sheep. This giant, this Philistine was no match for God, he told Saul, and *"God will deliver me out of his hand." (1 Samuel 17:37)* And if that wasn't enough, David had one more thing to reassure David of his own safety; he had a word from the Lord had **not** come to pass yet. He was to be king.

Look at David's response,

> *"You come at me with sword and spear and battle-axe. I come at you in the name of* GOD-*of-the-Angel-Armies, the God of Israel's troops, whom you curse and mock. This very day* GOD ***is handing you over to me***. *I'm about to kill you, cut off your head, and serve up your body and the bodies of your Philistine buddies to the crows and coyotes. The whole earth will know that there's an **extraordinary God** in Israel. And everyone gathered here will learn that* GOD *doesn't save by means of sword or spear. The battle belongs to* GOD—*he's handing you to us on a platter!"*
> **1 Samuel 17:45-47**

Wow!! Every time I read this I have to do the happy dance on the face of my enemies. What an amazing powerful declaration. God picked the right teenager to be king over Israel.

God, at times picks the underdog for various reasons. He will pick the weak in order to bring down the strong. He chooses the foolish to frustrate the wise. The unlearned are often chosen to humble the arrogant. And there are times when He uses the unskilled to teach the masters. Our enemy, the devil, knows this about God. Therefore he tries to convince us that our weaknesses bring our defeat. If we believe the lies and never gain faith in God, then he can trap us and spiritually keep us bound.

Goliath claimed victory over Israel because of David's size and age. What he saw was a puny nugget of flesh that was even smaller than his shield. Goliath towered almost three times over David's height. In his eyes he was the clear winner. Nevertheless, David used a small, insignificant, almost weightless pebble (so to speak) to bring the great Goliath down. I think that even if David had used five feathers, Goliath was going to go down. David's faith and willingness to put God at His word made him the victor already. All logic says that this was impossible, but God made it possible. David defied all odds and Heaven roared at the victory.

My favorite movie is, "The Lion, The Witch and the Wardrobe" by Disney. If you haven't seen this amazing movie, shame on you. The movie, of course, is an adaptation of the book written by C.S. Lewis under the same name. The story takes place during WWII where the four Pevensie children are sent away from the city into the countryside during the air raids for safety. They are placed in the home of a professor who has an enchanted wardrobe. After a number of things, the four children find themselves teleported to a new land called Narnia.

In this land there is a war going on, good versus evil and for a period of many years it seems like evil was winning. The

White Witch—who was the self proclaimed Queen—was a powerful, confident, intimidating woman (a depiction of Satan), has taken claim over Narnia and punishes any and all who stand against her. Meanwhile, in another part of the land, a gorgeous, larger than life lion named Aslan (a depiction of Jesus Christ) was happy about the arrival of the kids. In this land, there was a prophecy that one day four humans would come and help to restore balance again to Narnia and bring an end to the queen's reign. The four Pevensie children are completely unaware of all this and so begins their quest of learning who they are, what purpose they serve and how powerful they can be.

There are a number of scenes from the movie that get me every time. The first of these scenes takes place on their journey to find Aslan. With one of the brothers missing, the remaining three siblings are given weapons as gifts in preparation for the coming battle. Peter, the oldest of the children is given a sword and shield. His sister, Susan, did not agree with the gifts because in the real world swords were for warriors, not for teenage brothers like Peter.

They eventually find their way to Aslan's camp and soon discover more about this new land and the roles they play in it. This leads to my next favorite scene. Susan and Lucy are playing by a lake when all of a sudden they were in serious danger. Two ferocious wolves, servants of the White Witch, were sent to kill the children. Susan used one of the gifts she was given, a horn; which she used to call for help.

Those in the Aslan camp heard the girls cry for help and all the warriors, including Peter and Aslan, immediately came to their rescue. When they arrived, the girls had climbed a tree and the wolves were trying to attack them. Peter immediately drew his sword, which he had never used before, and pointed it in the faces of the wolves. Even though he was scared and unsure of himself, he held his ground. The wolves started to surround him, yet this young teenager could care less what happened to him; he was going to protect his sisters.

Out of nowhere, the powerful Aslan came out and slammed the wolf to the floor and pinning him down with one paw; evening the playing field for Peter.

Aslan's soldiers wanted to jump in to take out the second wolf, but he stopped them and told them this was Peter's fight. The wolf tried to intimidate Peter by telling him that he needed to put down the sword before someone got hurt, meaning Peter. He tried to make Peter doubt himself but Peter held his ground. Before he knew it the wolf leaped in the air towards Peter in an attempt to devour him. Peter's fate was not immediately known, as the wolf's body laid on top of him. To everyone's surprise, except Aslan, Peter was alive. He had plunged his sword into the body of the beast when it leaped towards him and with one blow, Peter killed the wolf.

Why does this scene touch me in such a way? It means a lot to me because Aslan was so majestic and powerful. You hear the strength just in the sound of his voice. Aslan was confident and inspiring when he spoke to Peter about his purpose and destiny. When Aslan pinned the first wolf down he showed that he could have gotten rid of the danger immediately. Instead he used that moment to help Peter learn and experience who Peter was for himself. Peter had to fight that battle in order to believe and have faith in Aslan's words. He needed to see that he could defy the odds against him. Aslan knew that some battles were required in order to help build confidence in the children. He knew what Peter and the others were capable of; he wanted them to know it for themselves. Even cooler, I believe, is that he showed them that when he was needed, he would be there to help even the playing field.

God does that to us friend. He allows His soldiers to face their fights and equips us for the battles ahead but He never leaves us alone to fight on an unfair battlefield. I've seen too many people run from the fight before them. Caught up in their own insecurities, inexperience, and fears they don't allow themselves to defy the odds. So many of us look at our enemy, acknowledge our weaknesses and run from the battlefield. We all want to have victories, but never want to be a part of the battle. We say that we trust God but when it all boils down to the truth, we don't trust Him.

At the end of the scene Aslan looks at Peter, tells him to clean his sword and kneel before Him. When Peter does, Aslan proudly announces, "Rise up, Sir Peter Wolf's-Bane, Knight of Narnia." How many times is our next promotion at the **end** of a fight but we give up before it is over? God wants to take so many of us to the next level, but we are too scared to defy the odds. We pray for God to take us to the next level and ask Him to set us free, but we're not willing to fight for it.

David might have been afraid when he walked into that valley to face Goliath, and if he was, David didn't allow his feelings of fear, or insecurity to dictate who was going to be the victor. After that declaration to Goliath in verses 45-47 of

1 Samuel 17, David swung his sling and let the pebble go. It is there that I believe God made the fight even. The scripture says that the rock was flung with such force that it sunk into Goliath's forehead. It probably broke through the skull and impacted his brain. He is stunned and falls down. After that David takes Goliath's own sword and cuts off the Philistines head.

When you look at yourself in the mirror what do you think about the reflection before you? Do you surround yourself with people who count you out instead of lifting you up? There is an enemy that would have you to believe that you are not worth it, but he is a liar; he actually fears what you might become. The reality is that God has designed everyone to have flaws and weaknesses. He does that so we can learn how to trust in Him. He also does it so that we can learn how to lean on each other for support and encouragement.

The heart of a soldier of God is not one who is fearless, but one who knows his God. He does not pretend to be all and know all. He is humble and recognizes his weaknesses. He does not count himself out when he is intimidated by what appears to be bigger and stronger. He has faith and has developed a relationship with his God. He will not let circumstances dictate his place and purpose. And he will trust that the Lord will never place upon him more than he can handle.

Do you have the heart of soldier?

CHAPTER EIGHT

Molding the Heart of a Soldier

Be *strong...*
When you are *weak.*
Be *brave...*
When you are *scared.*
Be *humble...*
When you are *victorious.*
Be a *warrior...*
Every single day.
-Anonymous

The anointed soldier...

What are some things that shapes the heart of a soldier towards God? Is it favor from man, riches of society or the power of authority? David had a heart after God but there were still things that God needed to fix and he would use certain circumstances to do so.

From David's life there is so much that we can learn. He made both good choices and bad ones. He displayed strong love and faith in God and yet, at times, did the exact opposite when he gave into temptation and fleshly desires. In David we see his courage in following God, but also his fear of a life without Him. His writings in the Psalms express his anger towards enemies and those who would rise up against his Lord; however they also express his passion and admiration for creation and the Creator. Through it all, in the good times and the bad, David was able to maintain favor with God. In fact, while Saul was still king, you could take the two of them and compare their differences.

Everything that David was, Saul was not. As David worshiped, Saul was tormented. Where David's fame grew, Saul's popularity was dwindling. It's no wonder that as their story continued, Saul grew to despise and even feel threatened by David. If you read their interactions carefully you can see that Saul liked and admired David which in turn made him hate David more. Saul's anger towards the young man was rooted in the fact that David was everything he wasn't. David did everything he could to honor and please his king. David fought for Saul bringing victory after victory. He would play music for Saul when the king felt ill and could not sleep. When given a task, David would complete it and even go above and beyond the task. He was almost perfect… and Saul hated him for it.

It's after David kills Goliath, where all of this begins. It started in small ways but Saul's jealousy was there. One of the most obvious times is found in 1 Samuel 18: 6-9, where the women come out to greet Saul with a song of victory after coming back from battle. As they sing, one of the lines of their songs to the king went on to say,

> *"Saul has slain his thousands, and David his tens of thousands."* **1 Samuel 18:7**

The scripture says that was a time of rejoicing quickly turned, for Saul, into a time of utter disgust.

> *"They have credited David with tens of thousands,"* he thought, *"but me with only thousands. What more can he get but the kingdom?"* **1 Samuel 18:8**

Saul immediately felt his throne threatened by David and from that point on, his mind tormented him. His jealousy grew so much that he hurled javelins at David while he played the harp. Verse 12 explains how Saul's jealousy grew to fear because, ***"the LORD was with David but had departed from Saul."*** In time Saul sought out ways to have David killed by setting him up to die in battle and when that failed, he eventually hunted David down himself. In the process Saul's blind anger was so great that it caused him to kill innocent priests, and even threatened the life of his own son Jonathan.

1 Samuel chapter 24 records a moment when Saul was on his quest to kill David and he went into a dark cave to relieve himself (use the bathroom). Unbeknownst to him, David and David's men were in the cave hiding. David's men recognized this as the perfect opportunity for David to end this war between

him and Saul. Instead of killing him, David just cuts off a piece of Saul's cloak. The Bible says that after he did this, David felt guilty.

He waited for Saul to leave the cave and then shouted out to him in order to show Saul he could have killed him but he chose mercy instead. That scene could have played out in a totally different way, but by all accounts it truly looked like God had offered Saul's life to David on a silver platter. Saul even acknowledged the fact in verse 18 saying, ***"the Lord delivered me into your hands, but you did not kill me."*** So, why? Why did David not take advantage of that moment and end this conflict once and for all? The answer is given by David a few verses before.

> *"This day you have seen with your own eyes how the Lord delivered you into my hands in the cave. Some urged me to kill you, but I spared you; I said, 'I will not lay my hand on my lord, because he is the Lord's anointed.'"* **1 Samuel 24:10**

It is possible that David looked ahead and thought to himself: *If I ever found myself in this position, is this how I would want to die?* After all, let's not forget, he was God's "anointed" as well. What if David later found himself in a place of sin, like Saul? Would he want his replacement to kill him in a cave like a dog while doing number two? Reading verses 11-15, David says plainly that God would judge between the two of them and he states to Saul, ***"may the Lord avenge the wrongs you have done to me, but my hand will not***

touch you. " He is leaving this all in God's hands and at the same time, tries to get answers as to why the king hates him so. Saul responds in tears and acknowledges that David has never wronged him. He admits that he can see why David will be king over Israel and asks him to spare his family when that day comes.

Don't get your feelings hurt

These two men both knew the same God. They both learned of God's ways and laws, but one made God's ways his heart's desire while the other just saw them as rules. One humbled himself before God and acknowledged that he lived to serve the Lord, while the other became greedy and arrogant believing that he could do as he pleased.

Sadly, as I look over my years in ministry, I have seen this same exact reflection in today's churches. So many believers have lost sight of mercy, grace, compassion, love and forgiveness. I am, at times, absolutely appalled at the behavior of some in the church when things do not happen the way that they demand it to be.

I have both seen and had my share of conflict with those in the world, but as an adult, the biggest and most outrageous conflicts I have witnessed were found in the very center of the church. I have seen ugly verbal arguments break out between board members and church members. I have watched a senior pastor so bent on revenge that after staff members had left, he called their new place of employment in order to discredit them to their new pastor; with hopes to get them fired. I have witnessed two young people break into a fight in the church simply because their parents were not speaking to one another.

The list of this stupidity goes on and on. I gather that one of the reasons why this world laughs at us is because leaders and pillars of the church wear their bitterness, envy and jealousy on their sleeve, planting seeds of hurt in the church while still asking for unbelievers to come to God. *Romans 2*: 22-24 says it well,

> *"You who say that one must not commit adultery, do you commit adultery? You who abhor idols, do you rob temples? You who boast in the law dishonor God by breaking the law. For, as it is written, 'The name of God is blasphemed among the Gentiles **because of you.**'"*

We are so quick to point out when someone is doing wrong, but we cease to see when we are doing wrong ourselves. ***"The name of God is blasphemed among the Gentiles because of you."*** Oh Lord forbid!!! I would never want it on my shoulders that I kept a non-believer from coming to the faith. But even amongst the believers, we point out adultery, fornication, dishonesty and immorality yet we miss our self-righteousness, judgmental, hypocritical behavior. And when one believer confronts another about these things, the latter becomes offended and accuses the first as being judgmental. Are believers not called to hold one another accountable and rebuke and correct for the safety of the church?

I like how the Message Bible words 1 Cor. 5: 9-13.

> *"I wrote you in my earlier letter that you shouldn't make yourselves at home among the sexually promiscuous. I didn't mean that you should have nothing at all to do with outsiders of that sort. Or with crooks, whether blue- or white-collar. Or with spiritual phonies, for that matter. You'd have to leave the world entirely to do that! But I am saying that* **you shouldn't act as if everything is just fine when a friend who claims to be a Christian is promiscuous or crooked, is flip with God or rude to friends, gets drunk or becomes greedy and predatory. You can't just go along with this, treating it as acceptable behavior.** *I'm not responsible for what the outsiders do, but don't we have some responsibility for those within our community of believers? God decides on the outsiders, but we need to decide when our brothers and sisters are out of line and, if necessary, clean house."*

Like David and Saul, there are many believers who worship the same God, but who follow Him in different ways. They sit in the same pews, sing the same songs and hear the same preaching, however respond and act in different ways. Churches are so busy fighting amongst themselves over attendance and carpet colors that they miss the foundational purpose of why they even exist, to help save the lost and encourage new believers to grow in truth. Most of all, we are here to show them love that is unconditional and always forgiving.

Love! This word gets thrown around so easily that its true meaning can be taken for granted. You see, it won't be by us standing on a crate on a busy city street or by posting scriptures on Facebook, Twitter and Instagram that lives will be won. These things may spark a conversation but the true winning of a soul comes from how believers live their lives. What makes us different than the rest? What is it that we offer that no one else can? True love! Pure, undeserving, unselfish, no strings attached, unconditional… love!

What happens sometimes to Christians though, is that we get duped into the pressures of society and we find ourselves speaking about God's love and forgiveness; in one moment but then name call and trash talk others the next. Our social media platforms become an avenue for condemning and name calling and we use the excuse of the freedom of expression to defend our actions not realizing we are defiling the more important testimony of the Spirit.

Recently, Sam spoke with an older gentleman who had rededicated his life to God after a number of years. The man mentioned one of the things that changed in his heart was the way he spoke to people. He said, "How could I grow closer to God and yet call another man an idiot and bash those in government authority? I may be upset at what I see, but that man is still someone who God loves. Normally this would be hard to do, but the more I read my Word and sought after Christ, the more I felt to pray for those whom I called names and bashed. This hit me more while I was in prayer, I heard God say to me, 'Who are you to call that man names? I forgave you and he is someone who I love just as I love you!' From that point on I knew I could not control what others do but I can control how I respond and how I prayed for them." Wow... just wow.

To love as Christ loved is not always going to be easy. Forgiveness is, for many, one of the hardest things to do. But as David said to Saul when he held up the piece of Saul's garment,

> *"Let the Lord judge between you and me, and let the Lord avenge me on you. But my hand shall not be against you. As the proverb of the ancients says, 'Wickedness proceeds from the wicked.' But my hand shall not be against you. After whom has the king of Israel come out? Whom do you pursue? A dead dog? A flea? Therefore let the Lord be judge, and judge between you and me, and see and plead my case, and deliver me out of your hand."* **1 Samuel 24:12-15 (NKJV)**

Someone can pose the argument, "Yeah, but David was not going to attack Saul because he was the king, so that's different than us." But the Bible does talk about respecting those in authority, honoring your husband and loving your wives. It speaks clearly about offending the brethren and leading a non-believer astray. Jesus spoke about the words that come out of our mouths and how we will be judged by them. We are warned not to gossip, backbite, slander and not discredit the scriptures by our actions and words. We are commanded to love our neighbors, clothe our enemies, and forgive those who trespass against us.

The list goes on and on. Whatever the reason and to whoever it is, the Bible covers all. If it does not threaten us in our worship and service to God we are told to love, respect, submit, pray for, be patient with, be kind to, turn the other cheek and sacrifice for the good of the Kingdom. (Whoever said that Christianity is a weak practice, they didn't know what true Christianity is.)

How does one become the compassionate and loving soldier God is asking us to become? There is no way that we can become that type of person on our own. How can I even look at someone without the feeling of anger if they hurt me? How is it possible to love someone that doesn't love me back? The answer is found in the sacrifice of our own pride. Take a moment to read, *I Peter 3:8-9 (NIV)*

When we are sympathetic to someone's random anger, or compassionate to someone who slips into sin and falls, that is when the world takes notice. Too many times we point a finger or judge those who have fallen short, however like David we have to consider that one day we may be in their shoes and how we treat people when they are in a state of weakness, is how we will be treated, if and when we are in the same place.

"Do not repay evil for evil." Am I the only one that thinks this is a difficult commandment? In my eyes, David had every right to kill Saul, but it is not my eyes that David was looking through. What keeps us from doing as David did? Unfortunately, we can be full of so much anger and frustration that when a conflict arises with our brothers and sister we can't even bring ourselves to greet them. We sit on the other side of the church and get others to rally with us.

For those people who want to justify and make excuses for their anger, bitterness, forgiveness, malicious, mean-spirited, evil behavior—let me just say it plainly—they are not called to be a soldier in the Army of the Lord. They make themselves vulnerable to being used by the enemy. In a battle they are a hindrances, a burden—and dare I say it—a handicap. We need to make a choice, whose side are we on and who do we choose to submit to?

David followed his heart and did not touch Saul. He had everyone around him telling him that killing Saul was right; consequently he knew that his God was not calling him to start his reign like this, so he obeyed. As I grew with the Lord I realized I was use to doing things the way I wanted to, if I felt it made sense then I did it without thinking and I had to face the repercussions later. I was not used to taking orders in life so I didn't consult God when I made my choices, but I have come to realize that the closer I get to Him the more I need His direction in life.

Real repentance touches the CO

There are several things King David will always be remembered for. He is known for killing the great Goliath, but he also is remembered for having an affair—using his power to rape her—with a woman named Bathsheba at the height of his reign *(2 Sam 11)*. There was a time when David was on top of his game; he was the king of Israel, undefeated, feared by other nations and shoulder deep in wealth. He had received a prophecy that his descendants would be on the throne forever and that his son would build the temple of God *(2 Sam 7)*. He was in his glory…but then he fell and fell hard. David raped Bathsheba, got her pregnant, killed her husband and covered it up. This was a great hit to David's ego and also his spiritual life. All of this was grounds for death, still there was one thing about David that was never seen in the lives of others—David knew how to **repent**; repent in a way that caught God's heart each time.

Think about this, Adam and Eve never repented (turn from their direction of sin) for disobeying God in the garden and eating the fruit. Cain never asked for forgiveness for killing Abel. Abraham did not apologize for not trusting God when he slept with Hagar or for when he lied to Pharaoh. Jacob did not ask for forgiveness for deceiving his father and brother. Aaron did not ask for forgiveness for leading the children into idolatry; Moses didn't even apologize for disobeying the Lord and striking the rock instead of speaking to it. That was not the character of David. David came to his senses. Look at what he says to Nathan the prophet, *"I have sinned against the* **Lord.** *"* Look at his apology to God and his prayer for mercy to God after these evil acts.

> *Create in me a pure heart, O God, and renew a steadfast spirit within me. Do not cast me from your presence or take your Holy Spirit from me. Restore to me the joy of your salvation and grant me a willing spirit, to sustain me.* **Psalms 51:10-12**

David knew that his heart had been blackened by his evil deeds—the same heart that was after God's heart—and he knew he could not move forward without cleansing it. I find David's request here so interesting, *"**Do not take your Holy Spirit from me.**"* Is it possible that David's request was from what he saw happen to Saul? According to 1 Sam 16: 14, God did remove His spirit.

> *"But the Spirit of the Lord departed from Saul, and a distressing spirit from the Lord troubled him."*

Even though the prophet had warned Saul that his actions would cause this, he did not listen, so God's presence was lifted from him. David was, however, pleading with God for this to not happen to him. He was now the anointed king in the cave deserving death—so to speak. Both Saul and David were spared, but it is David whose lineage remained. Why, all because he knew how to repent.

The heart of a soldier is the most precious thing to God and when it becomes corrupted, only God can renew it to make it whole again. My own heart goes out to David because his sin was for all to see. He did not fall privately; he fell publicly and rightfully so, he apologized publicly and privately to God. This man was not afraid of what people thought of him. Scripture records his servants and soldiers seeing him weep. When he rejoiced, his wife was embarrassed by him because he nearly danced his clothes off, 2 Samuel 6. (I kind of agree with her on that one.) But David did not care what others thought because his concern about his life was what God thought of him.

He knew the importance of repentance and if there is anything that David can teach us, this must be it. To repent means to feel remorse or regret and to change your mind concerning a past action. Repentance touches the heart of God and goes far because where the law demands death, God's mercy and grace comes in to cover our offense with His own blood.

I had to learn not to allow pride and arrogance to defeat me. Don't let it kick you out of the garden, like Adam and Eve or—in Abraham's case—produce an Ishmael. Don't allow your pride and frustrations to keep you from stepping foot into the Promised Land you so longed for. If you find yourself in a place of temptation, flee as Joseph did from Potiphar's wife.

But if you fall, which you might, be quick to admit you're wrong, repent from your ways and learn from your mistakes so that you can get back into the battle.

As we may admire David's legacy now, it stands to be said that his heart was molded by the conflicts of life, the betrayal of loved ones and mistakes that could not be reversed. Sometimes we think that warriors are made from strength, but sadly, strength is developed through the weakest moments of our lives.

CHAPTER NINE

Our Weapons of Warfare

"Soldiers when committed to a task, can't compromise. It's unrelenting devotion to the standards of duty and courage, absolute loyalty to others, not letting the task go until it's been done."
- Anonymous

My oldest son, Joey, is so precious to me—as most sons are to their mothers. I have watched him grow in so many ways. I've tried desperately to keep him small, but the laws of life won't allow for that. When he was a one year old, I started letting him watch two kiddy shows, Dora the Explorer and Blue's Clues. As he got older I knew that those shows would not be enough for his adventurous mind. My husband could not stand Dora. He hated that she shouted every time she spoke and was appalled by her lack of parenting supervision.

I, of course, played on his distaste for this cute little Mexican cartoon girl that roamed the dangerous forest without any parents just to get ice cream. Early one morning my kids came into our bedroom. I, myself, wasn't ready to get out of bed and neither was Sam. So I turned on the television and put Dora on while Sam was still sleeping.

I cracked up as it was very clear that this adorable little girl was invading his dreams. He woke up with a distorted face and looked at the T.V. just to see Dora singing one of her catchy tunes. Sam turned to me, who was completely amused by it all, and said, "You did that on purpose." I laughed so hard and teased him, a little too much.

When Joey was seven years old Sam knew that this had to stop, especially if he was going to keep his sanity. So he decided to have a father and son moment. He sat Joey down and made him watch Star Wars. "It is time for Joey to be a man," he declared. For a year or so he bought him Star Wars toys, made him watch Star Wars movies and taught him the wisdom of Yoda (a weird green frog lizard who talked backwards to sound more wise).

He even made strong spiritual connections as he warned our son of the dark side that ultimately became Dora the Explorer, not Darth Vader.

This stuck in Joey's head and he soon became fascinated with the light sabers (a laser sword for those who do not know about Star Wars). We bought one for him and also one for his sister, Rachel who was four years old at the time. Joey ended up chasing that poor girl around the yard yelling, "Fight with me!!" Unfortunately, all she did was run and scream. She, unlike her brother, wanted to go inside and watch Dora. Because of Joey's need for a sparring partner, Sam started sword fighting with him and Joey loved every minute of it.

As Joey grew older he wanted a stronger sword because those Toys R Us swords were bending and breaking with every battle my two Jedi's were having. Sam bought him a wooden sword, and then later on, an unbreakable synthetic sword. Soon Joey asked for a bow and arrow; somehow Sam convinced me and we got that. Not long after that he asked for a BB gun; someone gave us a rifle looking BB gun and Sam swore to monitor it. The day he asked for a knife was when mommy put her foot down and said, "Absolutely not!" I should have said no to the sword, but I guess that morning watching Dora pushed Sam too far.

I can say that Joey is a true soldier at heart. He is called to be a fighter and even though I tried to keep him in a world of cartoon explorers and blue dogs that had their own thinking chair, it was obvious that he had the heart of a fighter. As a warrior you don't have just one weapon, you have many and it takes time to learn how to use them all like Joey had to.

I watched as my husband taught my son the art of sword fighting and archery. They would do routines over and over until Joey got it and even after that he practiced to get even better and maintain his skills. There were times he came back inside with swollen fingers, cuts and bruises and one time with a bloody lip—we won't get into that one—it's still a sore spot.

But you know what? All this helped me to see how God has given us many weapons to use against our enemy. He has given us the Holy Scriptures, the Word of God itself. Through this "Sword" we learn about our enemy, our God, sin, a promise, creation, and our purpose. Additionally, it teaches us about other forms in which one develops and grows as well. In my journey of knowing God I remember learning about these other weapons that helped to strengthen me with the battles I faced and I want to share a few of them with you now.

It's not just music

One of the weapons that God has given us is the ability to worship. There are other forms of worship such as tithing, acts of service and so on. First, music is a foundational practice for just about every church. It, in itself, has an almost therapeutic power to help shape one's mood and emotions. You don't have to teach a child to lie or move to music. Start playing songs with a nice rhythm or beat next to a child or infant and watch them bounce and bop their heads. It is almost as if it is programmed in us to respond to music. It is used by every country and culture in some way as a way of history and tradition. The Bible makes mention of music in heaven and of how it is used as a form of praise to God.

The music industries of today, however have gone to great lengths to corrupt their listening audience with the lyrics they write and the videos they produce. I am blown away by the blatant sin and rebellion that is demonstrated in most mainstream modern music videos. In my home we are very strict about the music played in the house. We monitor the music that our kids have on their iPods and iPhones. Satan has taken music and has twisted it in ways that completely dishonors God. He knows that worship is one of the biggest weapons one can use against him. It is an element—in which it is believed—he knows very well.

> *"Thou hast been in Eden the garden of God; every precious stone was thy covering, the sardius, topaz, and the diamond, the beryl, the onyx, and the jasper, the sapphire, the emerald, and the carbuncle, and gold: the workmanship of thy tabrets and of thy pipes was prepared in thee in the day that thou wast created."*
> **Ezekiel 28:13**

The day that Lucifer (Satan's name before he fell from heaven) was created he had tambourines and pipes built in him. Many scholars believe that music came natural to him because of his design. Some go on to theorize that he led worship in heaven as a chief musician. Either way, music was a part of his makeup, it was a gift/talent. After his fall it became a talent he used to distract, confuse and distort man's relationship with God. The music created in this world through most of, if not all, the mainstream artists feed on the fleshly desires of man. It lures us in and imparts lies, and more filth into our souls.

God created forms of instruments in us as well. Think about it, in our English terms we call them "wind *pipes*", vocal "*chords*" and ear "*drums.*" Musical worship is a source of giving honor and expressing our love to God. Through song we vocalize our hearts towards Him and submit our will to His. Music inspires dancing that signifies a physical act of love and affection of God's mercy and provisions.

It was my love for worship music that inspired my desire for interpretive dance also known as Human Video. Though it is done today by the younger generation a bit differently than when I first did it, Human Video is pretty much an extension to the words of a song through visual dramatization. It gives movement to the words. Many of my struggles were fought while playing worship music. I made the declarations of some songs, my declarations. Songs of hope and His love became ways in which I found joy and the ability to move forward.

Praise is an outward and inward acknowledgment and admiration given to God. Though musical worship can be a form of that praise it can also be done in other ways. Scripture speaks of times when God's people would fall on their knees and worship him. They would make acknowledgments of who He was and how Great He is.

Kings of Israel, like Hezekiah, would take times of worship to ask God for forgiveness and mercy for the sin that they allowed to take over them. In 2 Chronicles 20, the Israelites gathered for war against their enemies, of Moab and Ammon. In verse 17 God spoke to the children of Israel and told them, *"You will not have to fight in this war."* How could they win if they didn't have to fight? There are times where God will tell you to just show up to the battle, but you won't have to do a thing because He will fight the battle for you.

In verse 18, after hearing the word of the Lord, the king and the inhabitants of Jerusalem along with the nation of Judah, worshiped the Lord. The battle had not taken place yet, still they believed God. When we get a word from the Lord saying that He will fight our battle—it does not matter how big or how numerous the enemy is—as you remain faithful to Him and His Word, you begin to show the true warrior in you.

Verse 22 shows that as the people began to worship the Lord in song and praises, their enemies ended up fighting amongst themselves and destroyed each other. The power of heeding the Word of God and worshiping Him in song and praise was so strong for Israel.

I have experienced it in my own life where He told me be still in the midst of my attacks and worship Him. He fought my battle for me. Likewise, I have seen how others, who chose to worship, instead of fighting naturally, achieved breakthroughs and victories in their situations. Marriages have been healed and friendships have been saved. Lies have been exposed and betrayals repaid.

Understand Your Orders

There is power in developing a personal relationship with God. This relationship looks different from person to person and is important in each one's development in battling the enemy. When you commune with God, you develop the opportunity to know Him and His plans for your life.

At a very young age I started hearing the voice of God. In my case, I did not seek out God, He sought me out. He spoke to me even when I had no desire to serve him. As I stated in my previous book, the young me wanted nothing to do with a "Father" persona of God and when God spoke to me I challenged his motives, but even in those moments, I learned God's voice. I was too young—and childlike—to complicate my conversations with God; I spoke to Him and still speak to Him as if He is my invisible friend. I don't talk about Him as if He is not in the room. I share everything with Him and I have learned the art of waiting on Him to speak back to me.

In my most desperate moments I have gone to God. When I was at the end of my rope, I begged Him not to stay silent. It was those moments that I needed to hear His voice the most. Many times I have been in a conflict where my flesh wants to rise up. I need God to tell me how to fight the battle because without His input, I would fight my enemies my own way.

David, again shows us exactly how to react when the enemy is upon us in

> *When the Philistines heard that David had been anointed king over Israel, they went up in full force to search for him, but David heard about it and went down to the stronghold. Now the Philistines had come and spread out in the Valley of Rephaim; so David inquired of the Lord, "Shall I go and attack the Philistines? Will you deliver them into my hands?"*
> **2 Samuel 5:17-19**

These verses show us a few things.

1. It shows us that Satan will wait for us to be in the place of promise before he attacks. The Philistines did not wait for David to get too comfortable in his position as king, before attacking him. There may be times when your greatest attacks come after your victory. It may come from a jealous competitor or in the shape of a friend. Whatever its form, know that the enemy never likes to see the

advancement of God's people for the Kingdom and will throw whatever he can to stop it's progression.

2. This story shows how stupid the enemy can really be. These Philistines were very familiar with David. When you really study the life of David you see that he was extremely close to the king of the Philistines. David was even going to be a bodyguard for that king when the Philistines were going to fight against the Israelites. They were very aware that David was the one who killed their champion Goliath years before. They knew him and knew the God he served. But, as David rose to this position, they followed with an act of foolish desperation. Listen, the enemy does know the God we serve, but he has hopes to trip us up, catch us off our guard and sneak up on us when he thinks we are not looking. He knows that he cannot win the war, but he will continue to try and take as many of us down with him.

3. Even though David defeated their champion Goliath years before, and he knew he had an army that would defeat them, he was not presumptuous. David humbled himself and asked God what *HE* wanted David to do. Let's look at the rest of the verse...

The Lord answered him, "Go, for I will surely deliver the Philistines into your hands."

David is successful and defeats the Philistines hands down. The coolest thing to note is that a few verses later in verse 23, the Philistines rise up again to attack David. David could have easily risen up against them like God had given him permission to do before, but instead he asks God again what he should do. That is an important thing to take note of. The battle looked no different. In fact the Philistines appeared to have mobilized the same exact way as before when David first encountered them. But David did not see this as the same thing; he saw it as a different occasion and sought God. Sure enough God had a different order to give about how to attack.

> *"Do not go straight up, but circle around behind them and attack them in front of the poplar trees. As soon as you hear the sound of marching in the tops of the poplar trees, move quickly, because that will mean the Lord has gone out in front of you to strike the Philistine army." So David did as the Lord commanded him, and he struck down the Philistines all the way from Gibeon to Gezer."* **2 Samuel 5:23-25**

When you develop a relationship with God, it is important that you follow His lead and not act out of your emotions. Don't be like Moses who struck the rock—as he had done before to produce water—but this time out of his frustration with the people of Israel. He was instructed the second time to speak to the rock and he lost sight of his orders. It is also important to understand that God may lead one person one way and you another, or that He may instruct you one way for one instance, but then another way in another instance.

Back to David and the Philistines, Satan likes to plays games, however God does not when it comes to his children. The second time God brought in the big guns—the "Uzis" as my mother would say—and sent his angels to defeat the Philistines for good. If I were in David's spot, I probably would not have inquired of the Lord the second time. I would assume that God would want me to do it the same way the second time as done the first time.

A few years ago my husband and I were asked to minister somewhere we had been before. Automatically we said yes because we loved the pastor and we wanted to do him the favor. But once we got there I didn't feel the anointing of God as I generally would have. The congregation was blessed, our friend was very pleased, but Sam and I knew that it just was not the same. The Lord spoke to me and said, "You must learn to pray about *everything*. Just because I allowed it once doesn't mean that I will allow it every time. Learn to consult me before you say yes or no to anything." That lesson was pivotal to my growth.

Likewise it will be pivotal to yours as well. Learn the voice of God for yourself so that as you move and operate you will know that you do so by His calling and His voice.

The weapon that satan fears most

Several years ago, Sam and I listened to a teaching on audio tape titled, "The Weapon Satan Fears the Most" by Perry Stone. In seeing a title like that, me being me, I needed to hear the story. While preparing to listen to this preaching we started talking a little bit on what it could be. We mentioned prayer, reading the word and maybe attending church. We were curious about what would be the weapon of our warfare that would be the most dangerous to Satan. As we sat there with our Bibles out and pens in hand, we listened intently to Perry Stone speak, he went through the very list we mentioned as important weapons but not the ultimate one.

In fact, Stone stated that going to church is **not** a weapon to say the least even though some of us think that it is. We believe that if we go regularly then we are in God's good graces and it keeps all the boogeymen away. Wrong.

Why would Satan care about you attending church? I may shock some of you when I say this, but Satan goes to church too. Some of you have probably seen his handiwork in your own churches. If you have attended church long enough, chances are you have witnessed splits and the falling of pastors and leadership. You know that that was not of God. He may have had to expose it but it was the enemy who distracted, manipulated, influenced and divided God's people.

I know there are many who may not agree with me on this, but reading the Bible is not the weapon he fears the most either. Though this is the Holy Word of God—to us who are believers—there are many atheists who have read the whole Bible back to front and can quote it better than most pastors. They have studied the scriptures probably more meticulously than most Christians and it doesn't make one hair stand up on Satan's arm. Satan himself is known to quote scripture for his own gain. If you don't believe me look as he quotes *Psalms 91:11,12* to Jesus while trying to tempt Him in *Matthew 4:6.*

Do you understand that Satan was not talking to Jesus about an event that happened? He wasn't talking about Adam and Eve, or Abraham and Moses. He wasn't recalling an event in time. The only reason he could quote this scripture is because he knew it, he read it. He didn't read the book we have in our hands; he was there as the ink was drying from the scribe's hands.

The crazy thing is that Satan not only quotes it, but he leaves parts out. He will do that to all of us. Satan will use the very scriptures that we so love and turn them against **us**, however how can he do that unless he reads and knows it. At this point you're probably thinking: *Well then wouldn't we have to know the Bible back and forth to be a threat?* Very true! Understand, I'm not saying that the Bible is **not** a weapon. It is an important one and one that we need, but what I'm saying, is that it's not the weapon **that is feared most**.

So if it's not going to church and it's not reading your word it must be praying!! Nope, sorry it's not that either. Prayer is something I do all the time. I find comfort in knowing that I have time with the Lord to intercede for my family and friends. Prayer has been the thing I have turned to when life was falling apart around me and I needed guidance. It's also been the thing that has given me strength during a very weak moment as I said before, still that too is not feared the most.

When Jesus came he had to set a lot of things right and one of them was about prayer. Read *Matt 6: 5-8*. So many people judge the strength of a person's walk by the way they pray and how long they pray. Jesus knew that the hypocritical religious leaders were taking prayer to a level that seemed impossible to the average believer. They prayed more than anyone except Jesus, but the way they prayed was not pleasing to God. I have seen the most outwardly spiritual person pray up a storm in church and walk out the doors of the church just to fall flat on their face. I know what some of you are thinking: *But does that mean prayer doesn't work? Does it mean we're never supposed to mess up after we pray?* The answer is, of course prayer works…anything used properly works. Of course you'll fall after a time of prayer. Don't lose sight of what the question is though…What weapon does Satan fear **THE MOST**.

As Perry Stone got into the meat of the message we were pleasantly surprised to hear what this grand weapon was. Sam and I knew the calling that God had for us was going to be great and we knew that the enemy was going to be on our heels trying to stop us. The answer to this question tickled our hearts so that we could learn of how to fight him during the process of what God had planned for us. We needed to get this because we were tired of always falling short and being beaten up.

So when Perry Stone finally got to the answer we were not expecting it to be what he said it was. According to Stone, the weapon Satan fears the most is…**obedience!!**

Yes that's it obedience!!

I know some of you are ready to debate or even challenge this, while for others, a light bulb just went off in your head. But this is the deadliest weapon we have at our fingertips if we in fact use it to its fullest capacity. It does not have to grow; there is no science to it. It's so simple that it's dramatically complicated. It is the simplicity of it that brings grown men to their knees in tears. It is the act of it that has allowed for the church to even exist to this day.

Let's get back to the matter of attending church, what good is going to church unless you obey the truth of the messages? We spoke on that already, but what about studying the Bible? I think reading about forgiveness is easier than actually obeying and forgiving an abuser, a murderer, or rapist. Reading about fleeing from youthful lust is easier than having to actually obey and stop looking at pornography. Reading what the scriptures say about not forsaking the fellowship of the church is a lot easier than obeying it and going to church every week. Sometimes we would rather stay home and watch some distant pastor on T.V. who doesn't hold us accountable to the bad choices we make.

Obedience sinful man raised a church

This very act, as simple as it seems is in fact the very thing we all have a problem doing. Let's get real for a minute, obedience doesn't seem like the thing Satan would be afraid of, right? Well let me tell you one of the most powerful stories that needed obedience. In *Acts chapter 10*, Simon Peter had been fasting for a while and started thinking about food. The Lord took the opportunity to give Simon Peter a lunch idea through a vision; however it was not the kind of lunch Simon Peter wanted. In the vision a sheet came down with only foods that the Jewish people called unclean: wild beast, creeping things and certain birds. To Simon Peter's horror the Lord said, *"Get up, Peter, kill and eat."* (verse 13) I always crack up with his answer,

"Surely not, Lord!" I love how he calls him "Lord" but tells him "no", the two words don't go together.

Simon Peter was not having it. In his mind, God had gone too far. Simon Peter tells God, "I have never eaten anything unclean," as if God didn't know that. Unfortunately, we are just like Simon Peter. God tells us to do something and immediately we tell God how His command is going to mess up God's own plan for our lives. The Lord goes on to tell Simon Peter that he is not to call anything that God has made unclean. This is not the amazing part, what is amazing is that God spoke to Peter **three times** and each time Simon Peter said, "no." Simon Peter was behaving as if it's about the food, but it was so much deeper than the food. The food was the best thing to use because he knew that Simon Peter was already starving from his fast.

God used this simple vision to help introduce the gospel to the gentiles. A gentile named Cornelius had sent some of his friends to Simon Peter's home to invite him to his house. He allowed these gentile men to stay in his home and then the next day went with them to the home of Cornelius.

Now, this very act was huge because a Jew did not enter the home of a gentile, let alone allow one to stay in his. According to the law, going into their home made the Jewish people unclean. That's why the Centurion understood if Jesus did not want to go into his home in *Matt 8:8*. In those days even if a gentile woman was in labor, Jews did not assist her because the last thing they wanted to do was bring another gentile in the world.

Peter was being obedient when God instructed him to go to Cornelius's home—here is when the miracle took place. For thousands of years the Jews thought that they were the chosen people of God, which they were, but they also felt that God only loved them. The Jews thought that because they circumcised their males and because they had Jewish blood in their veins, they were special and only they had access to God. At no point did Jews think that God was sending the Messiah to save the gentiles too; these were the thoughts of the disciples as well. To Peter's amazement, the power of God fell on Cornelius that day in front of his eyes and Cornelius starts speaking in tongues.

How could this happen? Simon Peter came to grips with the truth that God was not leaving anyone out of His blessings. His one act of **obedience**—even though it was against everything he believed in— to spread the gospel to others of all nationalities. It was because of this act from Simon Peter—that even though I am not a Jew—I am still a seed of Abraham and that goes for you as well. You and I are the products of this one act of obedience. Look at the result, we stand as one of the most powerful Armies against the gates of hell because of obedience.

The "gentile" church (anyone who is not a Jew) continues to be a growing entity that cannot be destroyed. No matter how we are persecuted, we just multiply. What if Peter stayed on the roof and kept fasting, would we be here? What if he kept building up his church, but excluding the needy, would we be here? What if he kept writing down the words of Jesus, but didn't obey them, would we be here? I don't want to know.

The fact remains, obedience is hard for weak minded, undisciplined, carnal followers. Some have gotten so used to lowering the standard of success in this war to mere reading, attendance and a five minute prayer to God as we run out the door; we have forgotten that victory in this battle requires so much more. The knowledge of God and his existence is not enough! We are called to *obey* His word, *obey* His commands and *obey* His laws. You can go to church all you want, but if you do not obey what you learn while attending, you are like a naked soldier in the middle of an active battlefield. You attended but have nothing to contribute. Satan fears those that can put the commands of their Commanding Officer over what he throws at them.

CHAPTER TEN

Knowing Your Enemy

Nobody loves the warrior
until the enemy is at the gate.
- Anonymous

It's Not a Dream...

One September morning my younger brother, came
into my room to tell me that James, our older brother,
was on the phone. I hadn't seen him since the year
after Sam and I had gotten married, so we were catching up.
Five months before his call I had my oldest son Joey. The time
was about 7:45 in the morning when we started talking, I was
telling him about his new nephew. I also shared with him the
serious step of faith I took when I turned in my resignation
to my job at the Chubb Institute in Manhattan, New York,
six-eight weeks earlier.

I loved my job and the people there. I had gained a lot
of favor with the administration and they were so great in
giving me the time I needed until I was ready to come back

to work after giving birth to Joey. I went through so much emotionally while I was pregnant and working. After giving birth, I was so tired and overwhelmed at the thought of leaving my son with someone else, so I decided to be a stay-at-home mom.

Towards the end of my pregnancy, to comfort myself, I would show up to work around 8:30-8:45 in the morning, go across the street and go underground to a little smoothie shop to buy a plain bagel, lightly toasted with melted butter and a banana and strawberry smoothie. My anxiety melted away as I enjoyed clocking in early, sitting at my desk and looking out the huge windows directly in front of my desk and diving into my pregnancy crave. I always wondered how the window washers had the courage to stand on those lifts to clean the windows of the adjacent buildings. Even though I enjoyed this view, I wish the building across the street was not blocking the view of the harbor just behind, it which was what I truly wanted to see. I thought that if I was able to look out at the water, that would top it all.

So there I was telling James just how much I enjoyed my job but I felt that I needed to be with Joey. In speaking with James I was thinking about going to visit my co-workers to introduce them to Joey. Near the end of the phone conversation with James, I heard my younger brother screaming from the living room, but I couldn't hear what he said. He started screaming again, but I was so engrossed in the last few words I was saying to James that I continued to ignore him. He finally busted in my room, grabbed the television remote and turned it on. "TURN ON THE TV!!" He yelled.

"What's wrong?" I said. To my horror the place I got my bagels and strawberry smoothies was on fire. A plane had just flown into the building that was part of my daily routine. The building was one of the two towers of the World Trade Center.

"Why is Manhattan on fire?" I asked shaking.

"That's what I have been trying to tell you" my brother said anxiously. I hung up with James and watched as the newscasters explained that a plane just hit one of the buildings. I grabbed the phone and started calling my job that was located in the Century Twenty One building on the fifteen-twenty first floor. I didn't know what to do other than try to contact my co-workers to make sure they were okay. No one answered. Then as my mind was just trying to wrap around the whole thing, I watched as a second plane flew into view on the T.V. screen and hit the second tower.

It was the second building that was just outside the view of my office window at work. This was the building that obstructed my view of the harbor. I so wanted to see when I worked there. Life paused for me for just a moment. I had no reaction and then my mind responded and I screamed out in pure fear while denial filled my world. I had never felt as powerless as I did in that moment; when all I could do was watch while this tragedy was unfolding before my eyes.

I called my friends again knowing full well no one was going to answer, but it was the only thing I was able to do in my shock. Then it got worse, I watched as pieces of the buildings began to fall and break off. "Those buildings are going down, they are not going to stand for much longer!!" My brother agreed.

Within ten minutes of me saying that, I watched on T.V. as the buildings that I had walked into for smoothies so many times, were falling like sandcastles being washed away by the tide, first one and then the other. What was going on? Why did this happen?

Shortly after the reports of the Twin Towers falling, there was a news broadcast that said another plane had hit the Pentagon, and not much later there was still another plane that had crashed in a remote area of Pennsylvania. By this time it was confirmed that this was a terrorist attack on the United States. I spent the whole day, like everyone else, in pure disbelief, where did these enemies come from and why were they attacking us? Who would do this? Why didn't we see this coming? Who could hate us this much that they would kill thousands and thousands of people? For the first time in my life I realized how small I really was. I knew that I needed God, but I didn't realize how much.

When your enemy shows his powers and might, it may cause you to doubt your own strength. I don't know about you, but that is when the need for God rises up even more for me.

I had to take Joey to his doctor's appointment that day and I found myself constantly looking in the sky for my invisible enemy. The need for shelter and safety gripped at my heart out of fear; fear that there would be more attacks.

Not all those responsible for this attack had died in the crash so there were more out there. Who were the people that attacked us? This was the question going through everyone's minds. Was it the Russians, the Chinese or the Iraqis?

I have one question for you...do you know the enemy you are fighting? Think about that question before you go any further. Do you know how he works? Do you know his goals? Do you know why he hates us so much? Do you know to what extent he will go to destroy you?

I am not an expert on the devil, we are not friends. I do not entertain him in my home or call him when I'm in need. I know him because I use to be his victim.

I am a firm believer in knowing your enemy and his capabilities for this spiritual war we are in. I think pastors and leaders cripple their members when they do not educate their congregants on the power of the enemy. We mention him quickly as if we are afraid he will appear if we talk too much about him. Maybe it's also with fear of giving him too much credit; I agree to an extent.

The danger of underestimating your enemy

I spoke about this briefly in my first book, it is foolish for us not to learn the schemes and tactics of the enemy. My mom says this to me all the time, "To be forewarned is to be forearmed." The enemy can use the simplest tactics and ways to have us fall into his trap. Many of us miss the small details and hints of his plans to have us fall. Paul speaks of how un-forgiveness can give Satan a hold over us...

> *"Anyone you forgive, I also forgive. And what I have forgiven—if there was anything to forgive—I have forgiven in the sight of Christ for your sake, in order that Satan might not outwit us. **For***

we are not unaware of his schemes."
2 Corinthians 2:10-11

That last sentence should come out of every soldier's mouth! God has provided us with the Bible that has exposed the blueprint of every filthy trap Satan could set for us. What excuse do we have, especially those in America? The Bible is written in several different versions, available online, digital and paperback. You can listen to it through multiple forms and platforms, but yet many will still find an excuse not to. We are fighting a very powerful enemy and at times I think we down play his powers.

I have heard preachers talk about Satan as if he was weak and wimpy, only *appearing* strong, but not having any real abilities. Listen, Satan is no match for God. That's like comparing the tiniest flea to the biggest of elephants. There is no comparison, but it does not mean he is without weapons. Remember the battle is not against God and Satan; God defeated him already. The battle is between man and Satan because we gave the enemy dominion over this earth and our lives. Now our everyday is retrieving what we gave away.

The battles we face day to day, are for us to decide if we will choose to walk with Christ or in the ways of the enemy. Just because we say a prayer at the altar does not mean we can walk into the enemy's territory completely invincible of his deceptive, crafty ways. It also doesn't mean that we can get as close to sin as we want without experiencing the consequences. Being in ministry for over several years, I have seen the fall of so many good men and women because they did not notice the enemy in his subtle way.

Lucifer was a very beautiful angel and an example of how creative and intentional God was in making his creations. Taking a closer look at *Ezekiel 28,* we see some things about this enemy. Between verses 12-19 we see a number of descriptions that many scholars agree are those of Satan. In verse 12 it says that he, Satan, was the **seal of perfection**. God made him completely perfect. There was not one flaw in Lucifer. There was no sin in him; there was no iniquity in him when God made him. He was **perfect in wisdom**. Where did he get that wisdom from? It was not worldly wisdom, it was only divine wisdom. He absorbed the teachings of God and had no one to corrupt him. He was anointed and ordained a guardian angel. God gave him a high position in this heavenly army. God allowed him to be on the holy mountain. He was to be admired by others. He was described as "blameless." The word blameless means that he was perfect, guiltless, irreproachable and virtuous. He was guiltless, perfect, irreproachable and virtuous **in his ways**.

As you can see, there is more to these verses than just these four points, but when you put it all together, perfect, wise, anointed, ordained, blameless, guiltless, it is hard to believe that these words once described the one we fight against today. What happened to this great creation? Read *verse 15b-17*

> "... **wickedness** *was found in you. Through your widespread trade you were filled with* **violence**, *and you* **sinned***. So I drove you in disgrace from the*

*mount of God, and I expelled you, guardian cherub, from among the fiery stones. Your heart became **proud** on account of your beauty, and you **corrupted** your wisdom because of your splendor. So I threw you to the earth;"*

He was perfect ***until*** wickedness was found in him. I have been in the church since I was 6 years old and serving the Lord since 11; I have never asked this question, but where did the wickedness come from in Lucifer? He was in heaven, there was no tree of knowledge of good and evil, there was no serpent to tempt him. How could wickedness be found in someone so perfect, who lived in a perfect world, serving a perfect God?

It goes on to say that violence filled him. How could a creation that was in an atmosphere of peace and serenity be full of violence? You have to remember that there was no war ever in heaven because God had no enemies so how did he know about war and violence?

It says that Lucifer sinned. From the beginning of it all, those created by God followed the Most High with love and admiration. No one knew what sin was because there was no reason to go against the rule of God. Somehow this blameless being was unhappy with what he was told and missed the mark God placed before him. Did God go to Lucifer—like he did to Cain in Genesis 4—and warn Lucifer to be careful because sin was knocking at ***his*** door? Whichever way, Lucifer did not fight the urge and he sinned against God without the need of a tree with forbidden fruit or a slithering reptile to entice him.

He looked at himself and started to admire his own beauty and the most dangerous ingredient was added to his character, pride. His admiration of himself corrupted his thinking. God gave him divine wisdom and he corrupted that wisdom. The sin of pride that was found in him was the most dangerous of all and sadly, this is found in us.

Pride is at the base of several sins. It's pride that can break up a family, destroy a marriage, bring down a company, demolish an empire, and level the future of a strong and powerful ministry. It is pride that makes us think we are above the law of sin and death. Pride is what makes us think we can touch what God has not given to us. It's even pride that allows us to think more highly of ourselves than we ought to. It is this sin that makes us think we can disobey the commands of our CO and have no consequences.

Is it not pride that keeps us from asking for forgiveness? Is it not pride that keeps us from asking for help when we know we are at the end of our rope? Isn't it pride that makes us believe that we can resist the opposite sex and not experience temptation? I question if it's even pride that makes us think that we can leave this life and go before God and expect entry into his holy Heaven when we have not surrendered our egos and hearts to Him.

After observing all these verses look at the end of this one,

"I threw you to the earth."

Not only was he thrown onto earth, but *Revelation 12:4* says that the dragon's tail swept 1/3 of the stars (angels) out of the sky and flung them to earth too. Satan was able to deceive 1/3 of angels to go against their leader. He convinced them, somehow, that he was more powerful and more capable of leading them than God Almighty. So not only was one perfect being in a perfect state corrupted by his own pride, he deceived an innumerable amount of perfect angels to follow him as well.

This cunning, conniving, sinful, deceptive, wicked, egotistical, prideful creature is our enemy. He is on earth invisible to our naked eye nevertheless we can see his handiwork every day. It was God's plan for us to have dominion over this beast and his fellow fallen comrades, however in the garden we handed over our authority to him, just like those angels did, and allowed him to deceive us. Just like a third of the angels, man chose to listen to Satan instead of following God.

The powerful deceptive nature of our enemy is seen the most in the book of Revelation. In Revelation chapter 20 the Bible says that before the complete end there will be a one thousand year reign of Christ. The only ones that remain will be the ones to survive the tribulation. These faithful believers will go through so much pain and struggle that the Bible says that if God does not shorten those days, humanity will not be able to survive according to *Matt 24:22*.

These people will have such a love for God that they would rather be beheaded than to allow themselves to get the mark of the beast. These amazing people are the ones that live to reign with Christ for one thousand years! Now these people are not reigning with Christ along with Satan still doing his same tricks. He is thrown into an abyss during this whole time so that he can't deceive. Let's just take a minute and pretend you are one of those special people that make it through that relentless time.

Imagine one thousand years serving God in this world without Satan. Also remember that those joining you are all like-minded. Their faith has already been tested for seven long years with extreme war, violence, poverty, wickedness, drug abuse, starvation and much more. They resisted all of that and have come out on the other side. Now, there is complete freedom to serve the Lord; no Satan, no deception, only God to worship with everything in us.

No schools to corrupt our children about evolution. No T.V. shows full of immorality, violence or profanity. All the music being played is uplifting and encouraging worship. Our kids are able to play outside freely because there is no danger or crime; basically no worries at all. We only need hospitals to bring our babies into the world because there won't be sickness as we know it now and we won't need orphanages or prisons anymore.

With an atmosphere of pure, uncorrupted worship, you would think that Satan's hold would be null and void. How could he deceive a nation, a people that survived his most brutal and violent attacks? How could he actually deceive a nation that had been saturated in the pure unrestrained presence, communication and goodness of God? How could he fool all of humanity a second time? Could Satan actually get any of us to turn against God that we have served faithfully for one thousand years? Well my friend he doesn't get one of those dedicated believers…but a number ***that can't be measured***.

*"When the thousand years are over, Satan will be released from his prison and will go out to deceive the nations in the four corners of the earth—Gog and Magog—and to gather them for battle. **In number they are like the sand on the seashore.** They marched across the breadth of the earth and surrounded the camp of God's people, the city he loves. But fire came down from heaven and devoured them."* **Revelation 20:7-9**

These people will know firsthand the strength of their enemy because they almost didn't make it, because of his relentless attacks. Can you believe that even in a perfect utopia where the people of God have no enemy, Satan is capable of getting us to turn against God, again? This is the kind of enemy we are fighting my friend. We can play games all we want and pretend, but in the end if we do not submit everything over to God we will find ourselves being the victim of an enemy who has been around since before the creation of this earth.

Take your enemy seriously

Scripture has many names for Satan. He is a liar and the father of lies, the prince of the power of this world, an accuser of the brethren and many more. There are a few things that Satan is not known for. He is not, however, called lazy, uncommitted, unmotivated, weak or distracted. He is not omnipresent like God, but between him and the other fallen angels, he has managed to create in this world a life that can seem God-less.

Going back to September 11th, it was said that there were hints of a hidden enemy planning an attack on America. Supposedly we were warned about their plans, but the threats weren't taken seriously. Sadly, thousands of lives were lost before we didn't take our enemies at their word. What would have happened if we believed the threats, then we would have protected ourselves more and possibly stopped them?

It is the same for us with our own hidden enemy. If we believed wholeheartedly that Satan existed, then we would not act the way we do. If we knew that Satan was real and hated us the way he truly does, we would not procrastinate in doing the commands of the Lord. We would not entertain and participate in anything that gives the slightest impression of his involvement.

So I leave this chapter with this question... Do you really know your enemy?

CHAPTER ELEVEN

No One Gets Left Behind

Here's a news flash: No soldier gives his life. That's not the way it works. Most soldiers who make a conscious decision to place themselves in harm's way, do it to protect their buddies. They do it because of the bonds of friendship – and it goes so much deeper than friendship.
- *Eric Massa*

SPOWs

The inspiration for this book on being a soldier, came in the oddest of ways. My friend Liz and I were going to the gym as faithfully as we possibly could. We were running on the treadmill, or should I say we were walking very fast on the treadmill, when I saw a certain news segment of a young man named Sergeant Bowe Bergdahl. He was a prisoner of war who had been rescued. President

Obama exchanged five Taliban prisoners for the life of this one soldier. It caused a serious division in the hearts of the American people because some members of Congress felt the President should have consulted with them about this decision.

I became very interested in this story because I thought there had to be something absolutely special about this young man; who was he and what was so special about him that the President of the United States would make this decision on his behalf. As I tried to follow the story from the T.V in the gym, there was a lot that was not making sense so I decided to follow the story at home for the next few days.

I expected to hear long words of love and admiration from his leaders and fellow troops, but I was even more confused as the opposite was expressed by others. In one news segment one of his fellow soldiers called him a traitor and a deserter because he didn't feel like Bergdahl deserve to be rescued. From his point of view Bergdahl abandoned his fellow troops. This fellow soldier expressed his anger even more when he explained that so many men risked their lives for a man who walked out on them. I could not have been more confused. Why would the President of the United States do such a controversial move for a man that deserted his fellow soldiers?

I felt compelled to find out more so I searched the Washington Post online and this is what I gathered. In 2009 Bergdahl was deployed to Afghanistan. While there, other Afghans observed him walking the streets and actually warned him that he was in a dangerous area. According to residents,

Bergdahl did not listen to them and just kept walking. After he left, there was a massive search all over the surrounding areas for this soldier, but he was not found.

Shortly after his disappearance, there were talks in the Obama administration of ways they could rescue this missing soldier. It was clear that he was now in the hands of the Taliban. After much talk of different ways they could retrieve this POW, President Obama agreed to release five Taliban commanders in exchange for Bergdahl. This act by the President was being scrutinized because many worried over the implications of this release.

After all was said and done, many more called Bergdahl a deserter and questioned his mental state and motives for walking off the base unarmed and into enemy territory. As they dug deeper, there were controversies around whether this soldier was actually even captured. Needless to say there was an onslaught of hateful twitter messages against this soldier. Brandon Friedman, an Army veteran, started to defend Bergdahl. His words defended that there was much we do not know about war and the state of mind that soldiers endure. I was so impressed and thankful that a veteran would stand up to the accusations and judgment this soldier experienced.

It was then that a spark ignited in my heart to go through this process again to write our second book on being a soldier in the service of our Lord. I wondered, "How many 'Spiritual POW's (Prisoners of War)' do we have in our churches today?" How many believers find themselves spiritually captured by the enemy's hands and find no hint of freedom? I don't know if Bowe really did leave his base and enter enemy territory unarmed and alone, or what his reasoning may have been. I was not there and I am not going to pass judgment where there needs to be mercy and love.

Likewise, there are many among us who find themselves as Spiritual Prisoners Of War and the last thing they need is judgment, ridicule and harassment. They require a time of healing and restoration and they need to be shown mercy and support.

A Spiritual Prisoner of War, (SPOW) can be seen in a number of ways. It can be those who seek to find a balance in living their lives as it seems fitting to them with God on the side— just enough to make them a "good" person. Another example is one who takes God's Word and translates it according to his/her way of life, picking and choosing what is right and what is wrong; what should be taken literal and what is figurative. Still some SPOWs can be those who are held as prisoners of their past, not finding freedom from choices they made and thinking that they are beyond redemption.

Basically a SPOW is one who does not find the true freedom in the salvation provided for all of us by the sacrifice of Jesus Christ. It is through salvation that we are given another chance to find purpose and meaning in this life through the guidance of the Holy Spirit. That salvation has provided a redirection for us to escape from the route we were headed in. The SPOW, however, will remain blinded by the enemy's lies and/or convictions. They will only see what their natural eyes see and not through the eyes of faith.

Alana

I recently celebrated my birthday. Now if you know me, I am not one to make a fuss over my birthday and my biggest desire is only to get a little gift from my hubby and a few kisses from each of my kids. One birthday I received something extra, a card in the mailbox from one of my most treasured friends, Alana. She started off the card with, "Girl, eighteen years of sisterhood! Where did the years go? We had an amazing friendship that has stood the test of time, trials and that has been through the fire; all for God's glory!!! It has been purified and made stronger. Such a true friend, my accountability partner!"

Alana and I met in Zion Bible Institute (now called North Point) in the second semester of my college years. I was immediately drawn to her and we connected so well. I was from NYC and those attending this school—were not. I was dealing with a culture shock in so many ways and I had only connected with a handful of people. Even in that handful, there were only a few I called friend. I already spent my 1st semester very lonely, especially since Sam was not with me. God had broken me down and revealed Himself to me in a lot of ways, but there was no one to share these experiences with.

I remember after winter break, I came back to the dorms and dropped my stuff in my room, greeted my roommate and then went downstairs to see some of the other girls. All of a sudden I saw a young lady walk through the door with her mother. Immediately she seemed different than the rest of the girls and—the cautious person that I was—I kept my distance. That distance lasted a very short while, especially since our campus was so small. I wasn't going to treat the new girl badly, so I introduced myself to her. I was glad I did because, we hit it off immediately. She was a beautiful Puerto Rican from a rough part of Connecticut. Her neighborhood and lifestyle was not that much different from mine. In fact, we found that we had a lot in common. We soon became fast friends—sisters I should say—and life on campus became more like home as I was emotionally adopted by her mom who was more adorable than I could imagine. Alana went to New York with me on spring break and met my family, she also met Sam's family and they fell in love with her as well.

We did everything together: prayed together, shared with each other, argued and most of all laughed with each other. Her and I laughed so much that it was just intolerable to the others on our dorm room floor. We were just obnoxiously happy at times and it became annoying to others. My favorite moments with Alana were when we would go into one of our rooms and sing worship songs. Her voice was angelic and intoxicating.

God used many moments like these to speak to both of us and prepare us for the calling He had on our lives. This was so important to two girls who were raised in scarcity and want. We had both been through abuse of some sort and needed God to change the direction society said we were destined to follow.

Then all of a sudden things changed; Alana's personality started to change; she started doing things that I did not think were right. She started to hang out with the wrong group of people, slacking off in her school work and even standing me up when we were suppose to go hang out. One day we had a huge fight when I confronted her about her behavior. I was tired of her using me and treating me like I was her second choice if her first choice did not pan out. She apologized, but I knew something else was wrong.

Alana stayed at Zion for a semester and a half before her finances became an issue. The expenses of the school became too much and she had to leave. It was like ripping my heart out the day she left. I loved her so much so we did not lose contact. We called each other and wrote letters to one another regularly. The friendship became stronger through the distance, to our surprise, but that made me miss her even more.

After leaving Zion she started working at Wendy's and met a guy who also worked there named Dale. One day she let me speak to this mystery man over the phone. He seemed like a nice guy, but there was something weird about him. He was sweet, but his sweetness seemed to have a bitter aftertaste. Alana found herself falling for him hard even though he was not a Christian. I warned her not to date someone who was unsaved, because her values would not be shared by his own, but that did not change anything.

Alana kept going with the relationship and she seemed happy but it just didn't sit well with me. My phone conversations became even harder for me to have with her because he now was on the phone with her every time we spoke. Dale would always pick up the second line and chime in on every little thing we spoke about. It made it impossible for me to speak to her freely.

One day I got a call from Alana, with Dale on the other line as usual, "Marsha, guess what?" Alana said with excitement. I knew immediately, "You better not tell me you got married."

She laughed nervously and said she had. They got married secretly at a city hall, without her mother's knowledge. *This was crazy*, I thought. What is she doing? This is not my Alana. Why was she doing this, but it was too late now. "Isn't that great Marsha?" Dale asked. I was anything but happy and all I wanted to do was tell her to get that creep off the phone so I could rip her in half. I was losing my sister and there was nothing I could do to stop it.

It wasn't too long after when she disconnected herself from all of our friends from Zion. Her conversations with me were becoming few and far between. The point where I lost it was when she backed out of coming to my wedding; where she was supposed to sing. Something was going on, she would never do this to me, nevertheless she had started to live her life very carelessly and the girl I loved and cared for was fading more and more. Eventually, she and I got into an argument and that was the one that ended it all. We stopped talking to each other and she changed her number. The only time I would hear from her after that was on her terms when she felt like calling me.

Five years came and went. Sam and I were married and we were in ministry for two or so years. Nearly every day I wondered about Alana; I wondered where she was and wanted desperately to tell her all of the good things that had been happening with us. I wanted to know how her and Dale were doing; did she have kids, what did they look like?

I was beside myself when I received a phone call and it was her. I didn't know what to say or think as I heard her voice over the phone. At first I wanted to be angry, but her voice softened me. Her and Dale were separated and she was the mother of 2 very young children. I didn't hesitate in getting her address so that I could do whatever I could to go see her.

Within a month of our first phone call, I got on the Greyhound bus to see her. When I arrived we embraced and immediately started catching up. As I entered her home I felt an extreme heaviness, it was a bit overwhelming but I wasn't really sure what it was.

It was on the second evening of my stay with her where I finally was able to talk to Alana about more than just the surface stuff. The Lord told me that Dale was physical with her. I saw in my spirit that he had beaten her, bouncing her off the walls. She admitted that he beat her so bad that she almost died. Alana confirmed my vision was real. She walked away and came back with a picture, "One day he and I had gotten into a fight and he started yelling at me." I listened as she told me of how the argument progressed and that at some point he took a crate and beat her in the face with it.

I was not prepared for what she was going to show me. The picture she showed me had her smiling with one of her eyes completely bloodshot. "This picture was taken almost two months *after* the beating. I was afraid I was going to lose my eye", she said to me. How bad was her eye before the two months? I was so beside myself. What had my sister gone through?

Apparently, after Alana got involved with Dale she found out that he was a criminal. Alana learned that he was on parole, but she didn't know to what extent of his conviction. Dale quickly became abusive and there was little she could do to get out of the relationship. He was determined to disconnect her from all of her friends and family and that's exactly what he did. He raped and choked her during her pregnancies and beat her till she almost blacked out. He even put a gun in her mouth and threatened to blow her head off if she ever came against him again.

In the last attack, she was able to escape to a neighbor's house, called the police and Dale was arrested. He was still in jail during my visit with her and she was doing whatever she could to put her life back together and keep him there.

We stayed in touch for a little under a year and Alana started getting herself back into things she should not have. She battled hard with getting her life in line with God. Alana wanted to serve Him, but did not know how to do it after her world had been destroyed. Soon she and I found ourselves arguing—again! She was making decisions, now, that placed her children in further danger. Alana praised me in one breath for being a friend that was real—raw and truthful—but those qualities were not welcomed in another breath when it was clear she was not living the life God intended her to live. She was making some of the same mistakes, and I could not stand by to watch her destroy her life all over again.

Alana was not happy with the things I was saying and for a second time she and I went our own ways. I wanted to stay by her but she didn't want to be saved from the life she was living. I was not going to approve of her choices; it wasn't okay in my eyes so she decided that it was best to leave once again. I felt so guilty for speaking up, but I remembered the last time she was heading in a wrong path and I kept silent. I did not know what was going to happen to our friendship; in my mind I had lost her for good.

Eight years, later through the wonders of Facebook, Alana and I reconnected once more. We made arrangements to talk on the phone and I was on edge on how this would turn out. When we started talking she admitted that the last eight years had been a struggle for her and her family. She shared that she and Dale were divorced, and he was still in jail. Alana admitted to me that before he went to jail he had gotten a fifteen year old girl pregnant.

They mainly arrested him for statutory rape and confiscated Alana's hard drive to see if there was any other evidence. It was there that they found out a lot more about her ex-husband. Let's just say that they didn't need her testimony of domestic violence to put him away for several years.

As the years went on her children got older and more things started to surface with them. Her daughter, Faith, who was three when her father was arrested, did not speak until after he was taken out of the home. It became evident that Dale had traumatized her daughter, but no one knew the extent, only Faith could tell us that story.

She needed to go through extensive counseling and it was in therapy that Faith told Alana about the abuse Dale inflicted on both her and her brother. When her son would misbehave, his father would lock him in the bathroom in the dark. Another time he purposely nicked him with a knife; this was going on when her son was only one year old. In these sessions Faith shared some unthinkable acts that the Dale had done. In hearing all this, Alana was in a wounded place, she was so tired, overwhelmed, broken and desperate; she had such a weight on her shoulders and she needed someone who would stand by her.

I will tell you, her challenges were not over, Alana was not the same. She was not the Alana I fell in love with, but she was finally willing to do whatever it took to be better than she was. Over the last several years Alana has allowed me to speak into her and Faith's life. Alana shared every moment of weakness that she has had and she told me when she has allowed her anger, fear, brokenness and addictions to dictate her decisions.

Even though she lives three hours away, I went toe to toe with her. I have challenged her thinking, pushed her to think outside the box and think beyond what she saw. I demanded the Alana, I knew was in there, to step forward and she took it. Alana didn't run as she had before. She did not turn to the things of this world as she had before.

I want to tell you that everything went smoothly. I want to say that God erased the consequences of her decisions, but sadly, I cannot. After years of not seeing each other, she brought her family to meet mine. Alana was tired, not a physical tiredness but clearly spiritual. I took her and Faith, now seventeen years old, out to talk with them privately because Faith was fighting Alana in every way.

Faith explained why her and her mother were not getting along and as they spoke, a verbal fight broke out. It was clear that there was so much hurt, pain and un-forgiveness that was bleeding into their relationship. Alana was trying to right her wrongs, but her daughter was bent on holding her prisoner for the choices she had made. Alana was angry at Faith because she saw herself in Faith and was trying desperately to keep history from repeating itself.

I took a hold of Alana and put her forehead on mine, I held her head in my hand, and asked her with tears in my own eyes, "How are you doing this?" It stopped her for a moment (Faith was still there). "How are you doing this my friend?" Tears willed up immediately in her eyes.

"I don't know." She whispered.

"You are so tired." I spoke softly.

"Yes." I put my hands on her cheeks as we both cried. "I'm trying so hard." She admitted.

"I know. I know." I held her, kissed her on her cheek and held her some more. I turned to Faith and hugged her. It was a healing moment as the two of them hugged each other. There was a lot more work but the walls of bitterness were down.

Today, Alana has plugged herself back into a healthy church and is the head worship leader there. Her daughter is on the team as well while her son plays the drums. Faith is pursuing her degree in psychology and Christian Counseling. After six years of praying, her fiancee finally gave his heart to the Lord and lastly, November 11, 2017 they got married after moving into their brand new home.

Alana and I are soon to celebrate twenty years of long distance friendship. I have to say that our relationship is the most God-ordained relationship I have. Distance hasn't broken us, sin hasn't devastated us, and offenses hasn't turned us. God has kept us. I tried not to judge her or condemn her and she trusted my harsh truth. I can tell you that the love and dedication I have for Alana is not something I could ever take credit for. The love I have for her is because of the God we both serve.

No one should be left behind

I think more of our fellow fallen brothers and sisters in this war would be able to survive this battle if they had someone carrying them.

> *For none of us lives for ourselves alone, and none of us dies for ourselves alone. If we live, we live for the Lord; and if we die, we die for the Lord. So, whether we live or die, we belong to the Lord. For this very reason, Christ died and returned to life so that he might be the Lord of both the dead and the living. You, then, why do you judge your brother or sister? Or why do you treat them with contempt? For we will all stand before God's judgment seat. Therefore let us stop passing judgment on one another. Instead, make up your mind not to put any stumbling block or obstacle in the way of a brother or sister.* **Romans 14:7-10, 13**

Look at your church for a minute and take an honest survey. Do you think your church welcomes the fallen brother? Does it embrace the SPOW? Is your church risking its life to retrieve the soldier captured by the enemy, or is it judgmental? Does it see brothers and sisters falling and yet remain silent, like I did in the beginning? Does it condemn the choices and judge the sinner without knowing all the truths like those people tweeting about Bowe Bergdahl?

Does your church understand that even the best of us will fall? Proverbs says that though the righteous *fall*, not once but, *seven* times rise again. *(Prov 27:16)* How is that even possible?

That means that even though I am clothed in God's rightness, I myself may very well be faced with this kind of weakness and failure, yet still I will rise again. It's the ***rising*** that makes us righteous. Anyone can fall, but it's the righteous that get back up.

> *Two are better than one,*
> *because they have a good return for their labor:*
> *If either of them falls down*
> **one can help the other up.**
> *But pity anyone who falls*
> *and* **has no one to help them up.**
> *Also, if two lie down together, they will keep warm.*
> *But how can one keep warm alone?*
> *Though one may be overpowered,*
> **two can defend themselves.**
> *A cord of three strands is not quickly broken.*
> **Ecclesiastes 4:9-12 (NIV)**

A righteous man can fall seven times and get up eight because he has another righteous man picking him up, defending him when the enemy attacks. The world has perfected criticism and ridicule when failure is present and sadly, many churches have adopted this point of view as well.

We are called to be different; we are to be the opposite. Take a minute to think, what would our churches look like if we fought for the SPOWs? What would they look like if we lifted up the fallen and celebrated the retrieval of the lost? Sometimes a soldier is who he is because another has stepped in to help in paving the way. We each have a part to play in the war and we need as many soldiers as possible to join the fight. If we help those who are SPOW's find freedom and understand true salvation, maybe we can be the light that this dark world is looking for.

"Out of every one hundred men, ten shouldn't even be there,
eighty are just targets, nine are the real fighters,
and we are lucky to have them, for they make the battle.
But the one, one is a warrior, and he will bring the others back."
-Heraclitus

CHAPTER TWELVE

We Already Have the Victory

*I am a soldier, I fight where I am told,
and I win where I fight*
-George S. Patton

From the very beginning of our relationship with each other, Sam and I have had the same taste for entertainment. We both enjoy movies and T.V. shows that blow things up, has superheroes and crazy action. In addition, we both enjoy playing video games till our fingers go numb. It's the best way to spend our time till Jesus comes. I think that it's also the secret to our happy marriage.

Unfortunately, he and I split ways when he started watching cars go round and round in a circle during NASCAR season. I find nothing entertaining in watching those cars go around in circles for 500 laps, it's too confusing. He and I adore watching the Olympics, but I am so irritated by the thought of watching sports of any kind.

One Sunday, I made an exception when we were invited to a Super Bowl party at a friend's house. Every year this woman from our church hosted the event with practically every member of our congregation there. After a few hours, I felt like it was getting late and my kids were starting to get tired. I told Sam that I was ready to leave, however he swore to me that it was almost over because there was only one minute left on the clock; everyone thought that it would be impossible for the offensive team to make a touchdown in that short amount of time.

I stood there holding our youngest child who had fallen asleep in my arms with my coat on ready to go. To my complete annoyance, this one minute **literally** lasted forty-five regular minutes. Every few seconds there was a sound of a buzzer because of tackles, penalties or time outs. I felt tricked as I started screaming at the T.V.—not because I was rooting for my favorite team but—because I just wanted to go home! To everyone's surprise, this team that everyone thought was not going to make it, made that unexpected touchdown! When this team finally made the touchdown I screamed, "Can I finally go home now??!!!"

Even though that period of time was extremely annoying for me I was able to learn something from this game. I remembered where the team was almost an hour before the win; it looked as if all hope was lost. I see the battle between the Satanic force and God's believers almost like a football game. Now I am not a football expert at all but follow and humor me here for a bit.

When on the "Field of Battle" in a football game you are either on the defense or offense. When on offense, one small mistake can turn over the direction of the game. One "fumble" or bad pass made, can find you quickly on the defensive. Where you were making strides to attack and score in the enemy's territory, now they are invading yours.

I can't help but parallel it to our spiritual walk. One moment we are victorious and making great strides against the enemy and the next—because of one careless step—we can find ourselves trying to protect our home from so unexpected invasion. I've seen many who began their salvation on the offensive side making strides and dodging obstacles, fumble the ball which forces them to play defense. That in itself is not a problem.

We all, from time to time, make mistakes. The power of how we play on this field of battle, however, is based on how well we gain back the possession of the ball. Sadly, many that I have seen, consistently find themselves *only* playing on defense.

Many believers are taught by their spiritual leaders how to defend and that is important, but—and I could be wrong here—very few are taught how to intercept the ball and turn the tide so that they can now attack. I believe that many ministers of the gospel sometimes portray our walk with God as if we are only supposed to be on the defensive side. Any good football coach will teach his team how to defend as well as how to score. Any good pastor or spiritual leader would do the same.

A few weeks ago I was having a talk with some of my friends and we started talking about the growing crisis with Isis. They were talking about what they had learned and how they were blown away by all of this. One of them said that she is praying that her and her kids just survive the violence. I felt differently. I said, "I am not raising victims, I am raising weapons. I am not raising my kids to survive; I am raising my kids to thrive." You see, I don't believe that my life as a Christian is meant for me to remain on the defensive. Shouldn't it be the other way around?

Take this Super Bowl game. The offensive team gained ground little by little. The other team did everything they could to keep their enemies from moving forward. There was just one minute left. But time slowed down as one minute turned into forty-five minutes. The offensive team would not accept defeat even when all else seemed to tell them otherwise.

After this amazing turn around, the news reported that many left the stadium already believing that the other team had won. I wonder, how many of us walk away too soon, believing that the "game" is over and had we just fought a little bit more we would have experienced a different result.

You know what also played an important part in this historical game? The offensive team's coaches. They were not stopping. They were talking on their headsets, writing on their boards, instructing their players and did everything to position their team for a win. They did all that they could to empower the team. Leaders, don't give up on those God has placed in their care. Don't just teach about defense and never about offense. Help those entrusted to you to give all they have till the very end. Listen, Satan knows that his time is short and he wants to keep as many of us as possible from scoring the final touchdown. It is on us to push forward.

A vision of victory...

Through a vision, God showed me a bit of what He had called me to do. I believed He did so because not too long after it I was faced with many hard trials. How I endured those trials would set the path for me on whether I would remain on defense or be able to go on offense.

It started with me being at the end of a dirt road in an abandoned junkyard like place; where everything was desolate and dark. The walk led me to a huge stone wall with a gate that was completely bolted shut. The gate was one that I had never seen before. The view on the other side was covered by mist and fog. I knew I was supposed to enter through it, but I didn't know how I was going to get through the locks.

Suddenly, a shadow was behind me. I could see it creeping up on me and before I knew it, the unknown creature lunged at me. In pure instinct, I drew my sword—which I didn't even know I had until that moment—and blocked every single blow thrown in my direction with no struggle. Even though the thing was straight on me, I still could not tell what it was.

I fought effortlessly, bringing fear into this strange creature, while shocking myself. I wielded my sword in such a way, that even I was lost in the moves. It felt like I knew the direction of each swing and thrust that was coming my way. The destruction of this creature was coming.

I realize that I wasn't the one needing to defend myself; this demon was. As the fight progressed my confidence raged more and I soon changed from blocking to being the one who was striking. The strength I possessed was far greater than this creature's. I swung my sword like a seasoned Jedi in Star Wars.

192| *The Makings of a Soldier*

It wasn't much longer until I defeated this demon; then my attention went back to the gate. As I approached it the second time, I now knew what this place was. This was the entrance to the gates of hell. I placed both hands on the gates and was expecting to open it but instead, I ripped the gates off of the stone walls as if they were Styrofoam.

As I stepped past the entrance, rage came over me. It mirrored my fighting years from when I was younger. A flood of memories from my childhood came over me and then it dawned on me I was here to take back what the devil stole from me. This was my battle to freedom.

My heart was beating with excitement and anticipation as I looked across the way and saw demon after demon charging after me. My hands gripped my sword as I swung it as hard and as fast as I could, making contact after contact. It was effortless as I went from one to another. I gained ground and confidence with every swing I swung.

Each swing felt as if I was slicing away days where I had locked myself in my room and cried from shame, pain of loneliness, the rejection from my father and others, hurt from the lies spoken over me, and the insecurities built up. Satan thought he had me when I was younger, but he would know now that I was free and that I survived so I be his worst nightmare.

As the battle went on I gathered they were not really fighting me but defending. They were trying to keep me from getting to something. They were hoping to push me back or tire me out. That wasn't happening as my spiritual adrenaline was pumping.

Then I saw on top of a hill that there were cages with human hands sticking out of them reaching out for help. I heard God say, "This fight was not just about you getting back what was taken from you, but it is to empower you to save those who are in those cages."

My "Field of Battle" was not just here but it stretched to where those people were. In those prisons were people that Satan had claimed as his. They were defeated and bound.

I quickly remembered my own cages. Even after salvation my mind was trapped in my failures, iniquities and incompetence. The difference between being trapped before salvation as opposed to after is that God unlocked the prison doors. I had to believe that I was able to leave. My prison just needed to be push open and I take that step of faith and walk out. God needed me to help them to believe that they could do what I just did—striking the enemy as a soldier—was going to depend on them.

I blew past every force that tried to keep me back and ran up the hill. I placed my hands on the doors of those prisons and, like Samson, I felt the power of God fill me as I ripped the doors off of every prison cell. The people in the cages were tired, dirty and anxious to leave. I turned around to lead them out… and the vision ended.

After it was all over my heart was beating out my chest. I was in tears and my adrenaline was going as if I was in the principal's office in middle school. I then heard God speak to me and say, "I am calling you to tear down the gates of hell and to go after those who the enemy thinks belong to him. This is what I created you for; you are a mighty Soldier. I have given you the authority to trample on snakes and scorpions and to overcome the power of the enemy. Nothing by any means will harm you. You will raise up an army for me and they will be dedicated, driven and ready for war. They are tired of hearing the wimpy, wishy-washy religion (yes God said "wishy-washy") preached to them. Satan is scared of them because he knows that once they realize who they really are, they threaten his very existence."

There is a story in the Bible that confirms God's words to me.

> *And I tell you that you are Peter, and on this rock I will build MY church, and the gates of Hades will not overcome it. I will give you the keys of the kingdom of heaven; whatever you bind on earth will be bound in heaven, and whatever you loose on earth will be loosed in heaven."* **Matthew 16:18-19 (NIV)**

Before this Simon Peter was just a fisherman who was asked to follow a carpenter. These words spoken to him changed everything. Jesus was telling Simon Peter who He was and who He would be. The name Peter means "rock or stone." Jesus goes on to say that on that rock he would build his church.

Was Peter jumping up and down in excitement about having the church built on his shoulders? The word, "church" was never spoken of before. Did Simon Peter even know what a "church" was? Did he understand the magnitude of this prophecy?

If Peter was the rock He would build His church on and we are the products of that, what authority was Jesus giving us? Look at the power given to us—He is giving us the keys to bind and loose. Do you understand what kind of power that is God is placing in the hands of His Army? We, the church, have the power and ability to tear down strongholds by the power given to us through ***His word***!! This one verse is just a sample given to us on where we should stand in this Field of Battle called life. Despite how Christianity is portrayed, we are not supposed to be hiding in a cave, waiting for the rapture to happen. We are instructed by our Commanding Officer to overtake the enemy's ground. And as we progress each day, we will continue to know that He will never leave us nor place us in situations that He has not equipped us to fight in. We are called for a purpose and given the weapons needed to move forward in taking back what was stolen from us.

Are you a soldier in the Army of God? Are you willing to trust your Commanding Officer? Are you willing to follow him on the battlefield? Will you commit to do whatever it takes to be victorious? Put aside the lies, your ego, your pride and recognize that the enemy we all fight—when we are without God—is smarter, more dedicated, stronger, and committed to his victory then we ever will be on our best day. He exist and with every passing day that you ignore his existence, you become weaker in your knowledge of the war you are in.

The only way to overcome the power of our enemy is to obey our Commanding Officer and let him mold us and make us into his weapon, his image, which is the true makings of a soldier.

SOLDIER

I am a soldier in the army of my God.
The Lord Jesus Christ is my Commanding Officer.
The Holy Bible is my code of conduct.
Faith, Prayer and the Word are my weapons of Warfare.
I have been taught by the Holy Spirit, trained by experience, tried by adversity and tested by fire.

I am a volunteer in this army, and I am enlisted for eternity.
I will either retire in this army at the rapture or die in this Army; but I will not get out, sell out, be talked out, or pushed out.

I am faithful, reliable, capable and dependable.
If my God needs me, I am there.
If He needs me in Sunday school, to teach children, work with the youth, help adults or just sit and learn. He can use me, because I am there.

I am a soldier. I am not a baby. I do not need to be pampered, petted, primed up, pumped up, picked up or pepped up.

I am a soldier. No one has to call me, remind me, write me, visit me, entice me or lure me.

I am a soldier. I am not a wimp.
I am in a place, saluting my King, obeying His orders, praising His name and building His Kingdom!
No one has to send me flowers, gifts, food, cards, candy or give me handouts.

I do not need to be cuddled, cradled, cared for or catered to.
I am committed.
I cannot have my feelings hurt bad enough to turn me around.
I cannot be discouraged enough to turn me aside.
I cannot lose enough to cause me to quit.

When Jesus called me into this army, I had nothing.
If I end up with nothing, I will still come out even. I will win.
My God will supply all my needs.
I am more than a conqueror. I will always triumph.
I can do all things through Christ.
Devils cannot defeat me.
People cannot disillusion me.
Weather cannot weary me.
Sickness cannot stop me.
Battles cannot beat me.
Money cannot buy me.
Governments cannot silence me and hell cannot handle me!

I am a soldier.
Even death cannot destroy me.
For when my commander calls me from this battlefield, He will promote
me to a captain and then bring me back to rule this world with Him.
I am a soldier, in this army, and I'm marching, claiming victory.
I will not give up. I will not turn around.
I am a soldier, marching heaven bound.
Here I stand! Will you stanßd with me?

-Anonymous

The Threshing: A Weapon Forged by Fire
is a survivor's story of severe physical, emotional and sexual abuse.
Marsha and Samuel Winters share her story of overcoming some
of the most traumatic abuse that a child could experience, leaving
her to battle with anger, sexual addiction, suicide and more. This
story is not just for those who have gone through issues as these.
This book is good for anyone who felt like life victimized them. In
this book you will see how God chases after the hurting, mends
the broken-hearted and restores what was stolen. God didn't just
remake her; he took Marsha's testimony and made it into a weapon
against the enemy and to set others free.

You can learn more about them on their website at
www.throughthewinters.com there you can read more inspirational
articles and sign up for their newsletters. You can purchase this
book at amazon.com or barnesandnobles.com.
ISBN: 9781498404266

CPSIA information can be obtained
at www.ICGtesting.com
Printed in the USA
BVHW07s2120160518
516408BV00004B/483/P